CLEP-23 COLLEGE-LEVEL EXAMINATION
PROGRAM SERIES

*This is your
PASSBOOK for...*

Principles of/ Introductory Marketing

*Test Preparation Study Guide
Questions & Answers*

NATIONAL LEARNING CORPORATION®

COPYRIGHT NOTICE

This book is SOLELY intended for, is sold ONLY to, and its use is RESTRICTED to individual, bona fide applicants or candidates who qualify by virtue of having seriously filed applications for appropriate license, certificate, professional and/or promotional advancement, higher school matriculation, scholarship, or other legitimate requirements of education and/or governmental authorities.

This book is NOT intended for use, class instruction, tutoring, training, duplication, copying, reprinting, excerption, or adaptation, etc., by:

1) Other publishers
2) Proprietors and/or Instructors of "Coaching" and/or Preparatory Courses
3) Personnel and/or Training Divisions of commercial, industrial, and governmental organizations
4) Schools, colleges, or universities and/or their departments and staffs, including teachers and other personnel
5) Testing Agencies or Bureaus
6) Study groups which seek by the purchase of a single volume to copy and/or duplicate and/or adapt this material for use by the group as a whole without having purchased individual volumes for each of the members of the group
7) Et al.

Such persons would be in violation of appropriate Federal and State statutes.

PROVISION OF LICENSING AGREEMENTS – Recognized educational, commercial, industrial, and governmental institutions and organizations, and others legitimately engaged in educational pursuits, including training, testing, and measurement activities, may address request for a licensing agreement to the copyright owners, who will determine whether, and under what conditions, including fees and charges, the materials in this book may be used them. In other words, a licensing facility exists for the legitimate use of the material in this book on other than an individual basis. However, it is asseverated and affirmed here that the material in this book CANNOT be used without the receipt of the express permission of such a licensing agreement from the Publishers. Inquiries re licensing should be addressed to the company, attention rights and permissions department.

All rights reserved, including the right of reproduction in whole or in part, in any form or by any means, electronic or mechanical, including photocopying, recording, or by any information storage and retrieval system, without permission in writing from the Publisher.

Copyright © 2025 by
National Learning Corporation

212 Michael Drive, Syosset, NY 11791
(516) 921-8888 • www.passbooks.com
E-mail: info@passbooks.com

PASSBOOK® SERIES

THE *PASSBOOK® SERIES* has been created to prepare applicants and candidates for the ultimate academic battlefield – the examination room.

At some time in our lives, each and every one of us may be required to take an examination – for validation, matriculation, admission, qualification, registration, certification, or licensure.

Based on the assumption that every applicant or candidate has met the basic formal educational standards, has taken the required number of courses, and read the necessary texts, the *PASSBOOK® SERIES* furnishes the one special preparation which may assure passing with confidence, instead of failing with insecurity. Examination questions – together with answers – are furnished as the basic vehicle for study so that the mysteries of the examination and its compounding difficulties may be eliminated or diminished by a sure method.

This book is meant to help you pass your examination provided that you qualify and are serious in your objective.

The entire field is reviewed through the huge store of content information which is succinctly presented through a provocative and challenging approach – the question-and-answer method.

A climate of success is established by furnishing the correct answers at the end of each test.

You soon learn to recognize types of questions, forms of questions, and patterns of questioning. You may even begin to anticipate expected outcomes.

You perceive that many questions are repeated or adapted so that you can gain acute insights, which may enable you to score many sure points.

You learn how to confront new questions, or types of questions, and to attack them confidently and work out the correct answers.

You note objectives and emphases, and recognize pitfalls and dangers, so that you may make positive educational adjustments.

Moreover, you are kept fully informed in relation to new concepts, methods, practices, and directions in the field.

You discover that you are actually taking the examination all the time: you are preparing for the examination by "taking" an examination, not by reading extraneous and/or supererogatory textbooks.

In short, this PASSBOOK®, used directedly, should be an important factor in helping you to pass your test.

NONTRADITIONAL EDUCATION

Students returning to school as adults bring more varied experience to their studies than do the teenagers who begin college shortly after graduating from high school. As a result, there are numerous programs for students with nontraditional learning curves. Hundreds of colleges and universities grant degrees to people who cannot attend classes at a regular campus or have already learned what the college is supposed to teach.

You can earn nontraditional education credits in many ways:
- Passing standardized exams
- Demonstrating knowledge gained through experience
- Completing campus-based coursework, and
- Taking courses off campus

Some methods of assessing learning for credit are objective, such as standardized tests. Others are more subjective, such as a review of life experiences.

With some help from four hypothetical characters – Alice, Vin, Lynette, and Jorge – this article describes nontraditional ways of earning educational credit. It begins by describing programs in which you can earn a high school diploma without spending 4 years in a classroom. The college picture is more complicated, so it is presented in two parts: one on gaining credit for what you know through course work or experience, and a second on college degree programs. The final section lists resources for locating more information.

Earning High School Credit

People who were prevented from finishing high school as teenagers have several options if they want to do so as adults. Some major cities have back-to-school programs that allow adults to attend high school classes with current students. But the more practical alternatives for most adults are to take the General Educational Development (GED) tests or to earn a high school diploma by demonstrating their skills or taking correspondence classes.

Of course, these options do not match the experience of staying in high school and graduating with one's friends. But they are viable alternatives for adult learners committed to meeting and, often, continuing their educational goals.

GED Program

Alice quit high school her sophomore year and took a job to help support herself, her younger brother, and their newly widowed mother. Now an adult, she wants to earn her high school diploma – and then go on to college. Because her job as head cook and her family responsibilities keep her busy during the day, she plans to get a high school equivalency diploma. She will study for, and take, the GED tests. Every year, about half a million adults earn their high school credentials this way. A GED diploma is accepted in lieu of a high school one by more than 90 percent of employers, colleges, and universities, so it is a good choice for someone like Alice.

The GED testing program is sponsored by the American Council on Education and State and local education departments. It consists of examinations in five subject areas: Writing, science, mathematics, social studies, and literature and the arts. The tests also measure skills such as analytical ability, problem solving, reading comprehension, and ability to understand and apply information. Most of the questions are multiple choice; the writing test includes an essay section on a topic of general interest.

Eligibility rules for taking the exams vary, but some states require that you must be at least 18. Tests are given in English, Spanish, and French. In addition to standard print, versions in large print, Braille, and audiocassette are also available. Total time allotted for the tests is 7 1/2 hours.

The GED tests are not easy. About one-fourth of those who complete the exams every year do not pass. Passing scores are established by administering the tests to a sample of graduating high school seniors. The minimum standard score is set so that about one-third of graduating seniors would not pass the tests if they took them.

Because of the difficulty of the tests, people need to prepare themselves to take them. Often, they start by taking the Official GED Practice Tests, usually available through a local adult education center. Centers are listed in your phone book's blue pages under "Adult Education," "Continuing Education," or "GED." Adult education centers also have information about GED preparation classes and self-study materials. Classes are generally arranged to accommodate adults' work schedules. National Learning Corporation publishes several study guides that aim to thoroughly prepare test-takers for the GED.

School districts, colleges, adult education centers, and community organizations have information about GED testing schedules and practice tests. For more information, contact them, your nearest GED testing center, or:

GED Testing Service
One Dupont Circle, NW, Suite 250
Washington, DC 20036-1163
1(800) 62-MY GED (626-9433)
(202) 939-9490

Skills Demonstration

Adults who have acquired high school level skills through experience might be eligible for the National External Diploma Program. This alternative to the GED does not involve any direct instruction. Instead, adults seeking a high school diploma must demonstrate mastery of 65 competencies in 8 general areas: Communication; computation; occupational preparedness; and self, social, consumer, scientific, and technological awareness.

Mastery is shown through the completion of the tasks. For example, a participant could prove competency in computation by measuring a room for carpeting, figuring out the amount of carpet needed, and computing the cost.

Before being accepted for the program, adults undergo an evaluation. Tests taken at one of the program's offices measure reading, writing, and mathematics abilities. A take-home segment includes a self-assessment of current skills, an individual skill evaluation, and an occupational interest and aptitude test.

Adults accepted for the program have weekly meetings with an assessor. At the meeting, the assessor reviews the participant's work from the previous week. If the task has not been completed properly, the assessor explains the mistake. Participants continue to correct their errors until they master each competency. A high school diploma is awarded upon proven mastery of all 65 competencies.

Fourteen States and the District of Columbia now offer the External Diploma Program. For more information, contact:

External Diploma Program
One Dupont Circle, NW, Suite 250
Washington, DC 20036-1193
(202) 939-9475

Correspondence and Distance Study

Vin dropped out of high school during his junior year because his family's frequent moves made it difficult for him to continue his studies. He promised himself at the time he dropped out that he would someday finish the courses needed for his diploma. For people like Vin, who prefer to earn a traditional diploma in a nontraditional way, there are about a dozen accredited courses of study for earning a high school diploma by correspondence, or distance study. The programs are either privately run, affiliated with a university, or administered by a State education department.

Distance study diploma programs have no residency requirements, allowing students to continue their studies from almost any location. Depending on the course of study, students need not be enrolled full time and usually have more flexible schedules for finishing their work. Selection of courses ranges from vo-tech to college prep, and some programs place different emphasis on the types of diplomas offered. University affiliated schools, for example, allow qualified students to take college courses along with their high school ones. Students can then apply the college credits toward a degree at that university or transfer them to another institution.

Taking courses by distance study is often more challenging and time consuming than attending classes, especially for adults who have other obligations. Success depends on each student's motivation. Students usually do reading assignments on their own. Written exercises, which they complete and send to an instructor for grading, supplement their reading material.

A list of some accredited high schools that offer diplomas by distance study is available free from the Distance Education and Training Council, formerly known as the National Home Study Council. Request the "DETC Directory of Accredited Institutions" from:

The Distance Education and Training Council
1601 18th Street, NW.
Washington, DC 20009-2529
(202) 234-5100

Some publications profiling nontraditional college programs include addresses and descriptions of several high school correspondence ones. See the Resources section at the end of this article for more information.

Getting College Credit For What You Know

Adults can receive college credit for prior coursework, by passing examinations, and documenting experiential learning. With help from a college advisor, nontraditional students should assess their skills, establish their educational goals, and determine the number of college credits they might be eligible for.

Even before you meet with a college advisor, you should collect all your school and training records. Then, make a list of all knowledge and abilities acquired through experience, no matter how irrelevant they seem to your chosen field. Next, determine your educational goals: What specific field do you wish to study? What kind of a degree do you want? Finally, determine how your past work fits into the field of study. Later on, you will evaluate educational programs to find one that's right for you.

People who have complex educational or experiential learning histories might want to have their learning evaluated by the Regents Credit Bank. The Credit Bank, operated by Regents College of the University of the State of New York, allows people to consolidate credits earned through college, experience, or other methods. Special assessments are available for Regents College enrollees whose knowledge in a specific field cannot be adequately evaluated by standardized exams. For more information, contact the Regents Credit Bank at:

Regents College
7 Columbia Circle
Albany, NY 12203-5159
(518) 464-8500

Credit For Prior College Coursework

When Lynette was in college during the 1970s, she attended several different schools and took a variety of courses. She did well in some classes and poorly in others. Now that she is a successful business owner and has more focus, Lynette thinks she should forget about her previous coursework and start from scratch. Instead, she should start from where she is.

Lynette should have all her transcripts sent to the colleges or universities of her choice and let an admissions officer determine which classes are applicable toward a degree. A few credits here and there may not seem like much, but they add up. Even if the subjects do not seem relevant to any major, they might be counted as elective credits toward a degree. And comparing the cost of transcripts with the cost of college courses, it makes sense to spend a few dollars per transcript for a chance to save hundreds, and perhaps thousands, of dollars in books and tuition.

Rules for transferring credits apply to all prior coursework at accredited colleges and universities, whether done on campus or off. Courses completed off campus, often called extended learning, include those available to students through independent study and correspondence. Many schools have extended learning programs; Brigham Young University, for example, offers more than 300 courses through its Department of Independent Study. One type of extended learning is distance learning, a form of correspondence study by technological means such as television, video and audio, CD-ROM, electronic mail, and computer tutorials. See the Resources section at the end of this article for more information about publications available from the National University Continuing Education Association.

Any previously earned college credits should be considered for transfer, no matter what the subject or the grade received. Many schools do not accept the transfer of courses graded below a C or ones taken more than a designated number of years ago. Some colleges and universities also have limits on the number of credits that can be transferred and applied toward a degree. But not all do. For example, Thomas Edison State College, New Jersey's State college for adults, accepts the transfer of all 120 hours of credit required for a baccalaureate degree – provided all the credits are transferred from regionally accredited schools, no more than 80 are at the junior college level, and the student's grades overall and in the field of study average out to C.

To assign credit for prior coursework, most schools require original transcripts. This means you must complete a form or send a written, signed request to have your transcripts released directly to a college or university. Once you have chosen the schools you want to apply to, contact the schools you attended before. Find out how much each transcript costs, and ask them to send your transcripts to the ones you are applying to. Write a letter that includes your name (and names used during attendance, if different) and dates of attendance, along with the names and addresses of the schools to which your transcripts should be sent. Include payment and mail to the registrar at the schools you have attended. The registrar's office will process your request and send an official transcript of your coursework to the colleges or universities you have designated.

Credit For Noncollege Courses

Colleges and universities are not the only ones that offer classes. Volunteer organizations and employers often provide formal training worth college credit. The American Council on Education has two programs that assess thousands of specific courses and make recommendations on the amount of college credit they are worth. Colleges and universities accept the recommendations or use them as guidelines.

One program evaluates educational courses sponsored by government agencies, business and industry, labor unions, and professional and voluntary organizations. It is the Program on Noncollegiate Sponsored Instruction (PONSI). Some of the training seminars Alice has participated in covered topics such as food preparation, kitchen safety, and nutrition. Although she has not yet earned her GED, Alice can earn college credit because of her completion of these formal job-training seminars. The number of credits each seminar is worth does not hinge on Alice's current eligibility for college enrollment.

The other program evaluates courses offered by the Army, Navy, Air Force, Marines, Coast Guard, and Department of Defense. It is the Military Evaluations Program. Jorge has never attended college, but the engineering technology classes he completed as part of his military training are worth college credit. And as an Army veteran, Jorge is eligible for a service that takes the evaluations one step further. The Army/American Council on Education Registry Transcript System (AARTS) will provide Jorge with an individualized transcript of American Council on Education credit recommendations for all courses he completed, the military occupational specialties (MOS's) he held, and examinations he passed while in the Army. All Army and National Guard enlisted personnel and veterans who enlisted after October 1981 are eligible for the transcript. Similar services are being considered by the Navy and Marine Corps.

To obtain a free transcript, see your Army Education Center for a 5454R transcript request form. Include your name, Social Security number, basic active service date, and complete address where you want the transcript sent. Mail your request to:
AARTS Operations Center
415 McPherson Ave.
Fort Leavenworth, KS 66027-1373

Recommendations for PONSI are published in *The National Guide to Educational Credit for Training Programs;* military program recommendations are in *The Guide to the Evaluation of Educational Experiences in the Armed Forces.* See the Resources section at the end of this article for more information about these publications.

Former military personnel who took a foreign language course through the Defense Language Institute may request course transcripts by sending their name, Social Security number, course title, duration of the course, and graduation date to:

Commandant, Defense Language Institute
Attn: ATFL-DAA-AR
Transcripts
Presidio of Monterey
Monterey, CA 93944-5006

Not all of Jorge's and Alice's courses have been assessed by the American Council on Education. Training courses that have no Council credit recommendation should still be assessed by an advisor at the schools they want to attend. Course descriptions, class notes, test scores, and other documentation may be helpful for comparing training courses to their college equivalents. An oral examination or other demonstration of competency might also be required.

There is no guarantee you will receive all the credits you are seeking – but you certainly won't if you make no attempt.

Credit By Examination

Standardized tests are the best-known method of receiving college credit without taking courses. These exams are often taken by high school students seeking advanced placement for college, but they are also available to adult learners. Testing programs and colleges and universities offer exams in a number of subjects. Two U.S. Government institutes have foreign language exams for employees that also may be worth college credit.

It is important to understand that receiving a passing score on these exams does not mean you get college credit automatically. Each school determines which test results it will accept, minimum scores required, how scores are converted for credit, and the amount of credit, if any, to be assigned. Most colleges and universities accept the American Council on Education credit recommendations, published every other year in the 250-page *Guide to Educational Credit by Examination*. For more information, contact:

The American Council on Education
Credit by Examination Program
One Dupont Circle, Suite 250
Washington, DC 20036-1193
(202) 939-9434

Testing programs:

You might know some of the five national testing programs by their acronyms or initials: CLEP, ACT PEP: RCE, DANTES, AP, and NOCTI. (The meanings of these initialisms are explained below.) There is some overlap among programs; for example, four of them have introductory accounting exams. Since you will not be awarded credit more than once for a specific subject, you should carefully evaluate each program for the subject exams you wish to take. And before taking an exam, make sure you will be awarded credit by the college or university you plan to attend.

CLEP (College-Level Examination Program), administered by the College Board, is the most widely accepted of the national testing programs; more than 2,800 accredited schools award credit for passing exam scores. Each test covers material taught in basic undergraduate courses. There are five general exams – English composition, humanities, college mathematics, natural sciences, and social sciences and history – and many subject exams. Most exams are entirely multiple-choice, but English composition exams may include an essay section. For more information, contact:

    CLEP
    P.O. Box 6600
    Princeton, NJ 08541-6600
    (609) 771-7865

ACT PEP: RCE (American College Testing Proficiency Exam Program: Regents College Examinations) tests are given in 38 subjects within arts and sciences, business, education, and nursing. Each exam is recommended for either lower- or upper-level credit. Exams contain either objective or extended response questions, and are graded according to a standard score, letter grade, or pass/fail. Fees vary, depending on the subject and type of exam. For more information or to request free study guides, contact:

    ACT PEP: Regents College Examinations
    P.O. Box 4014
    Iowa City, IA 52243
    (319) 337-1387
    (New York State residents must contact Regents College directly.)

DANTES (Defense Activity for Nontraditional Education Support) standardized tests are developed by the Educational Testing Service for the Department of Defense. Originally administered only to military personnel, the exams have been available to the public since 1983. About 50 subject tests cover business, mathematics, social science, physical science, humanities, foreign languages, and applied technology. Most of the tests consist entirely of multiple-choice questions. Schools determine their own administering fees and testing schedules. For more information or to request free study sheets, contact:

    DANTES Program Office
    Mail Stop 31-X
    Educational Testing Service
    Princeton, NJ 08541
    1(800) 257-9484

The AP (Advanced Placement) Program is a cooperative effort between secondary schools and colleges and universities. AP exams are developed each year by committees of college and high school faculty appointed by the College Board and assisted by consultants from the Educational Testing Service. Subjects include arts and languages, natural sciences, computer science, social sciences, history, and mathematics. Most tests are 2 or 3 hours long and include both multiple-choice and essay questions. AP courses are available to help students prepare for exams, which are offered in the spring. For more information about the Advanced Placement Program, contact:

    Advanced Placement Services
    P.O. Box 6671
    Princeton, NJ 08541-6671
    (609) 771-7300

NOCTI (National Occupational Competency Testing Institute) assessments are designed for people like Alice, who have vocational-technical skills that cannot be evaluated by other tests. NOCTI assesses competency at two levels: Student/job ready and teacher/experienced worker. Standardized evaluations are available for occupations such as auto-body repair, electronics, mechanical drafting, quantity food preparation, and upholstering. The tests consist of multiple-choice questions and a performance component. Other services include workshops, customized assessments, and pre-testing. For more information, contact:

NOCTI
500 N. Bronson Ave.
Ferris State University
Big Rapids, MI 49307
(616) 796-4699

Colleges and universities:

Many colleges and universities have credit-by-exam programs, through which students earn credit by passing a comprehensive exam for a course offered by the institution. Among the most widely recognized are the programs at Ohio University, the University of North Carolina, Thomas Edison State College, and New York University.

Ohio University offers about 150 examinations for credit. In addition, you may sometimes arrange to take special examinations in non-laboratory courses offered at Ohio University. To take a test for credit, you must enroll in the course. If you plan to transfer the credit earned, you also need written permission from an official at your school. Books and study materials are available, for a cost, through the university. Exams must be taken within 6 months of the enrollment date; most last 3 hours. You may arrange to take the exam off campus if you do not live near the university.

Ohio University is on the quarter-hour system; most courses are worth 4 quarter hours, the equivalent of 3 semester hours. For more information, contact:

Independent Study
Tupper Hall 302
Ohio University
Athens, OH 45701-2979
1(800) 444-2910
(614) 593-2910

The University of North Carolina offers a credit-by-examination option for 140 independent study (correspondence) courses in foreign languages, humanities, social sciences, mathematics, business administration, education, electrical and computer engineering, health administration, and natural sciences. To take an exam, you must request and receive approval from both the course instructor and the independent studies department. Exams must be taken within six months of enrollment, and you may register for no more than two at a time. If you are not near the University's Chapel Hill campus, you may take your exam under supervision at an accredited college, university, community college, or technical institute. For more information, contact:

Independent Studies
CB #1020, The Friday Center
UNC-Chapel Hill
Chapel Hill, NC 27599-1020
1(800) 862-5669 / (919) 962-1134

The Thomas Edison College Examination Program offers more than 50 exams in liberal arts, business, and professional areas. Thomas Edison State College administers tests twice a month in Trenton, New Jersey; however, students may arrange to take their tests with a proctor at any accredited American college or university or U.S. military base. Most of the tests are multiple choice; some also include short answer or essay questions. Time limits range from 90 minutes to 4 hours, depending on the exam. For more information, contact:

Thomas Edison State College
TECEP, Office of Testing and Assessment
101 W. State Street
Trenton, NJ 08608-1176
(609) 633-2844

New York University's Foreign Language Program offers proficiency exams in more than 40 languages, from Albanian to Yiddish. Two exams are available in each language: The 12-point test is equivalent to 4 undergraduate semesters, and the 16-point exam may lead to upper level credit. The tests are given at the university's Foreign Language Department throughout the year.

Proof of foreign language proficiency does not guarantee college credit. Some colleges and universities accept transcripts only for languages commonly taught, such as French and Spanish. Nontraditional programs are more likely than traditional ones to grant credit for proficiency in other languages.

For an informational brochure and registration form for NYU's foreign language proficiency exams, contact:

New York University
Foreign Language Department
48 Cooper Square, Room 107
New York, NY 10003
(212) 998-7030

Government institutes:

The Defense Language Institute and Foreign Service Institute administer foreign language proficiency exams for personnel stationed abroad. Usually, the tests are given at the end of intensive language courses or upon completion of service overseas. But some people – like Jorge, who knows Spanish – speak another language fluently and may be allowed to take a proficiency exam in that language before completing their tour of duty. Contact one of the offices listed below to obtain transcripts of those scores. Proof of proficiency does not guarantee college credit, however, as discussed above.

To request score reports from the Defense Language Institute for Defense Language Proficiency Tests, send your name, Social Security number, language for which you were tested, and, most importantly, when and where you took the exam to:

Commandant, Defense Language Institute
Attn: ATFL-ES-T
DLPT Score Report Request
Presidio of Monterey
Monterey, CA 93944-5006

To request transcripts of scores for Foreign Service Institute exams, send your name, Social Security number, language for which you were tested, and dates or year of exams to:

Foreign Service Institute
Arlington Hall
4020 Arlington Boulevard
Rosslyn, VA 22204-1500
Attn: Testing Office (Send your request to the attention of the testing office of the foreign language in which you were tested)

Credit For Experience

Experiential learning credit may be given for knowledge gained through job responsibilities, personal hobbies, volunteer opportunities, homemaking, and other experiences. Colleges and universities base credit awards on the knowledge you have attained, not for the experience alone. In addition, the knowledge must be college level; not just any learning will do. Throwing horseshoes as a hobby is not likely to be worth college credit. But if you've done research on how and where the sport originated, visited blacksmiths, organized tournaments, and written a column for a trade journal — well, that's a horseshoe of a different color.

Adults attempting to get credit for their experience should be forewarned: Having your experience evaluated for college credit is time-consuming, tedious work — not an easy shortcut for people who want quick-fix college credits. And not all experience, no matter how valuable, is the equivalent of college courses.

Requesting college credit for your experiential learning can be tricky. You should get assistance from a credit evaluations officer at the school you plan to attend, but you should also have a general idea of what your knowledge is worth. A common method for converting knowledge into credit is to use a college catalog. Find course titles and descriptions that match what you have learned through experience, and request the number of credits offered for those courses.

Once you know what credit to ask for, you must usually present your case in writing to officials at the college you plan to attend. The most common form of presenting experiential learning for credit is the portfolio. A portfolio is a written record of your knowledge along with a request for equivalent college credit. It includes an identification and description of the knowledge for which you are requesting credit, an explanatory essay of how the knowledge was gained and how it fits into your educational plans, documentation that you have acquired such knowledge, and a request for college credit. Required elements of a portfolio vary by schools but generally follow those guidelines.

In identifying knowledge you have gained, be specific about exactly what you have learned. For example, it is not enough for Lynette to say she runs a business. She must identify the knowledge she has gained from running it, such as personnel management, tax law, marketing strategy, and inventory review. She must also include brief descriptions about her knowledge of each to support her claims of having those skills.

The essay gives you a chance to relay something about who you are. It should address your educational goals, include relevant autobiographical details, and be well organized, neat, and convey confidence. In his essay, Jorge might first state his goal of becoming an engineer. Then he would explain why he joined the Army, where he got hands-on training and experience in developing and servicing electronic equipment.

This, he would say, led to his hobby of creating remote-controlled model cars, of which he has built 20. His conclusion would highlight his accomplishments and tie them to his desire to become an electronic engineer.

Documentation is evidence that you've learned what you claim to have learned. You can show proof of knowledge in a variety of ways, including audio or video recordings, letters from current or former employers describing your specific duties and job performance, blueprints, photographs or artwork, and transcripts of certifying exams for professional licenses and certification – such as Alice's certification from the American Culinary Federation. Although documentation can take many forms, written proof alone is not always enough. If it is impossible to document your knowledge in writing, find out if your experiential learning can be assessed through supplemental oral exams by a faculty expert.

Earning a College Degree

Nontraditional students often have work, family, and financial obligations that prevent them from quitting their jobs to attend school full time. Can they still meet their educational goals? Yes.

More than 150 accredited colleges and universities have nontraditional bachelor's degree programs that require students to spend little or no time on campus; over 300 others have nontraditional campus-based degree programs. Some of those schools, as well as most junior and community colleges, offer associate's degrees nontraditionally. Each school with a nontraditional course of study determines its own rules for awarding credit for prior coursework, exams, or experience, as discussed previously. Most have charges on top of tuition for providing these special services.

Several publications profile nontraditional degree programs; see the Resources section at the end of this article for more information. To determine which school best fits your academic profile and educational goals, first list your criteria. Then, evaluate nontraditional programs based on their accreditation, features, residency requirements, and expenses. Once you have chosen several schools to explore further, write to them for more information. Detailed explanations of school policies should help you decide which ones you want to apply to.

Get beyond the printed word – especially the glowing words each school writes about itself. Check out the schools you are considering with higher education authorities, alumni, employers, family members, and friends. If possible, visit the campus to talk to students and instructors and sit in on a few classes, even if you will be completing most or all of your work off campus. Ask school officials questions about such things as enrollment numbers, graduation rate, faculty qualifications, and confusing details about the application process or academic policies. After you have thoroughly investigated each prospective college or university, you can make an informed decision about which is right for you.

Accreditation

Accreditation is a process colleges and universities submit to voluntarily for getting their credentials. An accredited school has been investigated and visited by teams of observers and has periodic inspections by a private accrediting agency. The initial review can take two years or more.

Regional agencies accredit entire schools, and professional agencies accredit either specialized schools or departments within schools. Although there are no national accrediting standards, not just any accreditation will do. Countless "accreditation associations" have been invented by schools, many of which have no academic programs and sell phony degrees, to accredit themselves. But 6 regional and about 80 professional accrediting associations in the United States are recognized by the U.S. Department of Education or the Commission on Recognition of Postsecondary Accreditation. When checking accreditation, these are the names to look for. For more information about accreditation and accrediting agencies, contact:

>Institutional Participation Oversight Service Accreditation and State Liaison Division
>U.S. Department of Education
>ROB 3, Room 3915
>600 Independence Ave., SW
>Washington, DC 20202-5244
>(202) 708-7417

Because accreditation is not mandatory, lack of accreditation does not necessarily mean a school or program is bad. Some schools choose not to apply for accreditation, are in the process of applying, or have educational methods too unconventional for an accrediting association's standards. For the nontraditional student, however, earning a degree from a college or university with recognized accreditation is an especially important consideration. Although nontraditional education is becoming more widely accepted, it is not yet mainstream. Employers skeptical of a degree earned in a nontraditional manner are likely to be even less accepting of one from an unaccredited school.

Program Features

Because nontraditional students have diverse educational objectives, nontraditional schools are diverse in what they offer. Some programs are geared toward helping students organize their scattered educational credits to get a degree as quickly as possible. Others cater to those who may have specific credits or experience but need assistance in completing requirements. Whatever your educational profile, you should look for a program that works with you in obtaining your educational goals.

A few nontraditional programs have special admissions policies for adult learners like Alice, who plan to earn their GEDs but want to enroll in college in the meantime. Other features of nontraditional programs include individualized learning agreements, intensive academic counseling, cooperative learning and internship placement, and waiver of some prerequisites or other requirements – as well as college credit for prior coursework, examinations, and experiential learning, all discussed previously.

Lynette, whose primary goal is to finish her degree, wants to earn maximum credits for her business experience. She will look for programs that do not limit the number of credits awarded for equivalency exams and experiential learning. And since well-documented proof of knowledge is essential for earning experiential learning credits, Lynette should make sure the program she chooses provides assistance to students submitting a portfolio.

Jorge, on the other hand, has more credits than he needs in certain areas and is willing to forego some. To become an engineer, he must have a bachelor's degree; but because he is accustomed to hands-on learning, Jorge is interested in getting experience as he gains more technical skills. He will concentrate on finding schools with strong cooperative education, supervised fieldwork, or internship programs.

Residency Requirements

Programs are sometimes deemed nontraditional because of their residency requirements. Many people think of residency for colleges and universities in terms of tuition, with in-state students paying less than out-of-state ones. Residency also may refer to where a student lives, either on or off campus, while attending school.

But in nontraditional education, residency usually refers to how much time students must spend on campus, regardless of whether they attend classes there. In some nontraditional programs, students need not ever step foot on campus. Others require only a very short residency, such as one day or a few weeks. Many schools have standard residency requirements of several semesters but schedule classes for evenings or weekends to accommodate working adults.

Lynette, who previously took courses by independent study, prefers to earn credits by distance study. She will focus on schools that have no residency requirement. Several colleges and universities have nonresident degree completion programs for adults with some college credit. Under the direction of a faculty advisor, students devise a plan for earning their remaining credits. Methods for earning credits include independent study, distance learning, seminars, supervised fieldwork, and group study at arranged sites. Students may have to earn a certain number of credits through the degree-granting institution. But many programs allow students to take courses at accredited schools of their choice for transfer toward their degree.

Alice wants to attend lectures but has an unpredictable schedule. Her best course of action will be to seek out short residency programs that require students to attend seminars once or twice a semester. She can take courses that are televised and videotape them to watch when her schedule permits, with the seminars helping to ensure that she properly completes her coursework. Many colleges and universities with short residency requirements also permit students to earn some credits elsewhere, by whatever means the student chooses.

Some fields of study require classroom instruction. As Jorge will discover, few colleges and universities allow students to earn a bachelor's degree in engineering entirely through independent study. Nontraditional residency programs are designed to accommodate adults' daytime work schedules. Jorge should look for programs offering evening, weekend, summer, and accelerated courses.

Tuition and Other Expenses

The final decisions about which schools Alice, Jorge, and Lynette attend may hinge in large part on a single issue: Cost. And rising tuition is only part of the equation. Beginning with application fees and continuing through graduation fees, college expenses add up.

Traditional and nontraditional students have some expenses in common, such as the cost of books and other materials. Tuition might even be the same for some courses, especially for colleges and universities offering standard ones at unusual times. But for nontraditional programs, students may also pay fees for services such as credit or transcript review, evaluation, advisement, and portfolio assessment.

Students are also responsible for postage and handling or setup expenses for independent study courses, as well as for all examination and transcript fees for transferring credits. Usually, the more nontraditional the program, the more detailed the fees. Some schools charge a yearly enrollment fee rather than tuition for degree completion candidates who want their files to remain active.

Although tuition and fees might seem expensive, most educators tell you not to let money come between you and your educational goals. Talk to someone in the financial aid department of the school you plan to attend or check your library for publications about financial aid sources. The U.S. Department of Education publishes a guide to Federal aid programs such as Pell Grants, student loans, and work-study. To order the free 74-page booklet, *The Student Guide: Financial Aid from the U.S. Department of Education,* contact:

    Federal Student Aid Information Center
    P.O. Box 84
    Washington, DC 20044
    1 (800) 4FED-AID (433-3243)

Resources

Information on how to earn a high school diploma or college degree without following the usual routes is available from several organizations and in numerous publications. Information on nontraditional graduate degree programs, available for master's through doctoral level, though not discussed in this article, can usually be obtained from the same resources that detail bachelor's degree programs.

National Learning Corporation publishes study guides for all of these exams, for both general examinations and tests in specific subject areas. To order study guides, or to browse their catalog featuring more than 5,000 titles, visit NLC online at www.passbooks.com, or contact them by phone at (800) 632-8888.

Organizations

Adult learners should always contact their local school system, community college, or university to learn about programs that are readily available. The following national organizations can also supply information:

    American Council on Education
    One Dupont Circle
    Washington, DC 20036-1193
    (202) 939-9300

Within the American Council on Education, the Center for Adult Learning and Educational Credentials administers the National External Diploma Program, the GED Program, the Program on Noncollegiate Sponsored Instruction, the Credit by Examination Program, and the Military Evaluations Program.

College-Level Examination Program (CLEP)

1. WHAT IS CLEP?

CLEP stands for the College-Level Examination Program, sponsored by the College Board. It is a national program of credit-by-examination that offers you the opportunity to obtain recognition for college-level achievement. No matter when, where, or how you have learned – by means of formal or informal study – you can take CLEP tests. If the results are acceptable to your college, you can receive credit.

You may not realize it, but you probably know more than your academic record reveals. Each day you, like most people, have an opportunity to learn. In private industry and business, as well as at all levels of government, learning opportunities continually occur. If you read widely or intensively in a particular field, think about what you read, discuss it with your family and friends, you are learning. Or you may be learning on a more formal basis by taking a correspondence course, a television or radio course, a course recorded on tape or cassettes, a course assembled into programmed tests, or a course taught in your community adult school or high school.

No matter how, where, or when you gained your knowledge, you may have the opportunity to receive academic credit for your achievement that can be counted toward an undergraduate degree. The College-Level Examination Program (CLEP) enables colleges to evaluate your achievement and give you credit. A wide range of college-level examinations are offered by CLEP to anyone who wishes to take them. Scores on the tests are reported to you and, if you wish, to a college, employer, or individual.

2. WHAT ARE THE PURPOSES OF THE COLLEGE-LEVEL EXAMINATION PROGRAM?

The basic purpose of the College-Level Examination Program is to enable individuals who have acquired their education in nontraditional ways to demonstrate their academic achievement. It is also intended for use by those in higher education, business, industry, government, and other fields who need a reliable method of assessing a person's educational level.

Recognizing that the real issue is not how a person has acquired his education but what education he has, the College Level Examination Program has been designed to serve a variety of purposes. The basic purpose, as listed above, is to enable those who have reached the college level of education in nontraditional ways to assess the level of their achievement and to use the test results in seeking college credit or placement.

In addition, scores on the tests can be used to validate educational experience obtained at a nonaccredited institution or through noncredit college courses.

Some colleges and universities may use the tests to measure the level of educational achievement of their students, and for various institutional research purposes.

Other colleges and universities may wish to use the tests in the admission, placement, and guidance of students who wish to transfer from one institution to another.

Businesses, industries, governmental agencies, and professional groups now accept the results of these tests as a basis for advancement, eligibility for further training, or professional or semi-professional certification.

Many people are interested in the examination simply to assess their own educational progress and attainment.

The college, university, business, industry, or government agency that adopts the tests in the College-Level Examination Program makes its own decision about how it will use and interpret the test scores. The College Board will provide the tests, score them, and report the results either to the individuals who took the tests or the college or agency that administered them. It does NOT, and cannot, award college credit, certify college equivalency, or make recommendations regarding the standards these institutions should establish for the use of the test results.

Therefore, if you are taking the tests to secure credit from an institution, you should FIRST ascertain whether the college or agency involved will accept the scores. Each institution determines which CLEP tests it will accept for credit and the amount of credit it will award. If you want to take tests for college credit, first call, write, or visit the college you wish to attend to inquire about its policy on CLEP scores, as well as its other admission requirements.

The services of the program are also available to people who have been requested to take the tests by an employer, a professional licensing agency, a certifying agency, or by other groups that recognize college equivalency on the basis of satisfactory CLEP scores. You may, of course, take the tests SOLELY for your own information. If you do, your scores will be reported only to you.

While neither CLEP nor the College Board can evaluate previous credentials or award college credit, you will receive, with your scores, basic information to help you interpret your performance on the tests you have taken.

3. WHAT ARE THE COLLEGE-LEVEL EXAMINATIONS?

In order to meet different kinds of curricular organization and testing needs at colleges and universities, the College-Level Examination Program offers 35 different subject tests falling under five separate general categories: Composition and Literature, Foreign Languages, History and Social Sciences, Science and Mathematics, and Business.

4. WHAT ARE THE SUBJECT EXAMINATIONS?

The 35 CLEP tests offered by the College Board are listed below:

COMPOSITION AND LITERATURE:
- American Literature
- Analyzing and Interpreting Literature
- English Composition
- English Composition with Essay
- English Literature
- Freshman College Composition
- Humanities

FOREIGN LANGUAGES
- French
- German
- Spanish

HISTORY AND SOCIAL SCIENCES
- American Government
- Introduction to Educational Psychology
- History of the United States I: Early Colonization to 1877
- History of the United States II: 1865 to the Present
- Human Growth and Development
- Principles of Macroeconomics
- Principles of Microeconomics
- Introductory Psychology
- Social Sciences and History
- Introductory Sociology
- Western Civilization I: Ancient Near East to 1648
- Western Civilization II: 1648 to the Present

SCIENCE AND MATHEMATICS
- College Algebra
- College Algebra-Trigonometry
- Biology
- Calculus
- Chemistry
- College Mathematics
- Natural Sciences
- Trigonometry
- Precalculus

BUSINESS
- Financial Accounting
- Introductory Business Law
- Information Systems and Computer Applications
- Principles of Management
- Principles of Marketing

CLEP Examinations cover material taught in courses that most students take as requirements in the first two years of college. A college usually grants the same amount of credit to students earning satisfactory scores on the CLEP examination as it grants to students successfully completing the equivalent course.

Many examinations are designed to correspond to one-semester courses; some, however, correspond to full-year or two-year courses.

Each exam is 90 minutes long and, except for English Composition with Essay, is made up primarily of multiple-choice questions. Some tests have several other types of questions besides multiple choice. To see a more detailed description of a particular CLEP exam, visit www.collegeboard.com/clep.

The English Composition with Essay exam is the only exam that includes a required essay. This essay is scored by college English faculty designated by CLEP and does not require an additional fee. However, other Composition and Literature tests offer optional essays, which some college and universities require and some do not. These essays are graded by faculty at the individual institutions that require them and require an additional $10 fee. Contact the particular institution to ask about essay requirements, and check with your test center for further details.

All 35 CLEP examinations are administered on computer. If you are unfamiliar with taking a test on a computer, consult the CLEP Sampler online at www.collegeboard.com/clep. The Sampler contains the same tutorials as the actual exams and helps familiarize you with navigation and how to answer different types of questions.

Points are not deducted for wrong or skipped answers – you receive one point for every correct answer. Therefore it is best that an answer is supplied for each exam question, whether it is a guess or not. The number of correct answers is then converted to a formula score. This formula, or "scaled," score is determined by a statistical process called *equating*, which adjusts for slight differences in difficulty between test forms and ensures that your score does not depend on the specific test form you took or how well others did on the same form. The scaled scores range from 20 to 80 – this is the number that will appear on your score report.

To ensure that you complete all questions in the time allotted, you would probably be wise to skip the more difficult or perplexing questions and return to them later. Although the multiple-choice items in these tests are carefully designed so as not to be tricky, misleading, or ambiguous, on the other hand, they are not all direct questions of factual information. They attempt, in their way, to elicit a response that indicates your knowledge or lack of knowledge of the material in question or your ability or inability to use or interpret a fact or idea. Thus, you should concentrate on answering the questions as they appear to be without attempting to out-guess the testmakers.

5. WHAT ARE THE FEES?

The fee for all CLEP examinations is $55. Optional essays required by some institutions are an additional $10.

6. WHEN ARE THE TESTS GIVEN?

CLEP tests are administered year-round. Consult the CLEP website (www.collegeboard.com/clep) and individual test centers for specific information.

7. WHERE ARE THE TESTS GIVEN?

More than 1,300 test centers are located on college and university campuses throughout the country, and additional centers are being established to meet increased needs. Any accredited collegiate institution with an explicit and publicly available policy of credit by examination can become a CLEP test center. To obtain a list of these centers, visit the CLEP website at www.collegeboard.com/clep.

8. HOW DO I REGISTER FOR THE COLLEGE-LEVEL EXAMINATION PROGRAM?

Contact an individual test center for information regarding registration, scheduling and fees. Registration/admission forms can also be obtained on the CLEP website.

9. MAY I REPEAT THE COLLEGE-LEVEL EXAMINATIONS?

You may repeat any examination providing at least six months have passed since you were last administered this test. If you repeat a test within a period of time less than six months, your scores will be cancelled and your fees forfeited. To repeat a test, check the appropriate space on the registration form.

10. WHEN MAY I EXPECT MY SCORE REPORTS?

With the exception of the English Composition with Essay exam, you should receive your score report instantly once the test is complete.

11. HOW SHOULD I PREPARE FOR THE COLLEGE-LEVEL EXAMINATIONS?

This book has been specifically designed to prepare candidates for these examinations. It will help you to consider, study, and review important content, principles, practices, procedures, problems, and techniques in the form of varied and concrete applications.

12. QUESTIONS AND ANSWERS APPEARING IN THIS PUBLICATION

The College-Level Examinations are offered by the College Board. Since copies of past examinations have not been made available, we have used equivalent materials, including questions and answers, which are highly recommended by us as an appropriate means of preparing for these examinations.

If you need additional information about CLEP Examinations, visit www.collegeboard.com/clep.

THE COLLEGE-LEVEL EXAMINATION PROGRAM

How The Program Works

CLEP examinations are administered at many colleges and universities across the country, and most institutions award college credit to those who do well on them. The examinations provide people who have acquired knowledge outside the usual educational settings the opportunity to show that they have learned college-level material without taking certain college courses.

The CLEP examinations cover material that is taught in introductory-level courses at many colleges and universities. Faculties at individual colleges review the tests to ensure that they cover the important material taught in their courses. Colleges differ in the examinations they accept; some colleges accept only two or three of the examinations while others accept nearly all of them.

Although CLEP is sponsored by the College Board and the examinations are scored by Educational Testing Service (ETS), neither of these organizations can award college credit. Only accredited colleges may grant credit toward a degree. When you take a CLEP examination, you may request that a copy of your score report be sent to the college you are attending or plan to attend. After evaluating your scores, the college will decide whether or not to award you credit for a certain course or courses, or to exempt you from them. If the college gives you credit, it will record the number of credits on your permanent record, thereby indicating that you have completed work equivalent to a course in that subject. If the college decides to grant exemption without giving you credit for a course, you will be permitted to omit a course that would normally be required of you and to take a course of your choice instead.

What the Examinations Are Like

The examinations consist mostly of multiple-choice questions to be answered within a 90-minute time limit. Additional information about each CLEP examination is given in the examination guide and on the CLEP website.

Where To Take the Examinations

CLEP examinations are administered throughout the year at the test centers of approximately 1,300 colleges and universities. On the CLEP website, you will find a list of institutions that award credit for satisfactory scores on CLEP examinations. Some colleges administer CLEP examinations to their own students only. Other institutions administer the tests to anyone who registers to take them. If your college does not administer the tests, contact the test centers in your area for information about its testing schedule.

Once you have been tested, your score report will be available instantly. CLEP scores are kept on file at ETS for 20 years; and during this period, for a small fee, you may have your transcript sent to another college or to anyone else you specify. (Your scores will never be sent to anyone without your approval.)

APPROACHING A COLLEGE ABOUT CLEP

The following sections provide a step-by-step approach to learning about the CLEP policy at a particular college or university. The person or office that can best assist students desiring CLEP credit may have a different title at each institution, but the following guidelines will lead you to information about CLEP at any institution.

Adults returning to college often benefit from special assistance when they approach a college. Opportunities for adults to return to formal learning in the classroom are now widespread, and colleges and universities have worked hard to make this a smooth process for older students. Many colleges have established special service offices that are staffed with trained professionals who understand the kinds of problems facing adults returning to college. If you think you might benefit from such assistance, be sure to find out whether these services are available at your college.

How to Apply for College Credit

STEP 1. Obtain the General Information Catalog and a copy of the CLEP policy from the colleges you are considering. If you have not yet applied for admission, ask for an admissions application form too.

Information about admissions and CLEP policies can be obtained by contacting college admissions offices or finding admissions information on the school websites. Tell the admissions officer that you are a prospective student and that you are interested in applying for admission and CLEP credit. Ask for a copy of the publication in which the college's complete CLEP policy is explained. Also get the name and the telephone number of the person to contact in case you have further questions about CLEP.

At this step, you may wish to obtain information from external degree colleges. Many adults find that such colleges suit their needs exceptionally well.

STEP 2. If you have not already been admitted to the college you are considering, look at its admission requirements for undergraduate students to see if you can qualify.

This is an important step because if you can't get into college, you can't get college credit for CLEP. Nearly all colleges require students to be admitted and to enroll in one or more courses before granting the students CLEP credit.

Virtually all public community colleges and a number of four-year state colleges have open admission policies for in-state students. This usually means that they admit anyone who has graduated from high school or has earned a high school equivalency diploma.

If you think you do not meet the admission requirements, contact the admissions office for an interview with a counselor. Colleges do sometimes make exceptions, particularly for adult applicants. State why you want the interview and ask what documents you should bring with you or send in advance. (These materials may include a high school transcript, transcript of previous college work, completed application for admission, etc.) Make an extra effort to have all the information requested in time for the interview.

During the interview, relax and be yourself. Be prepared to state honestly why you think you are ready and able to do college work. If you have already taken CLEP examinations and scored high enough to earn credit, you have shown that you are able to do college work. Mention this achievement to the admissions counselor because it may increase your chances of being accepted. If you have not taken a CLEP examination, you can still improve your chances of being accepted by describing how your job training or independent study has helped prepare you for college-level work. Tell the counselor what you have learned from your work and personal experiences.

STEP 3. Evaluate the college's CLEP policy.

Typically, a college lists all its academic policies, including CLEP policies, in its general catalog. You will probably find the CLEP policy statement under a heading such as Credit-by-Examination, Advanced Standing, Advanced Placement, or External Degree Program. These sections can usually be found in the front of the catalog.

Many colleges publish their credit-by-examination policies in a separate brochure, which is distributed through the campus testing office, counseling center, admissions office, or registrar's office. If you find a very general policy statement in the college catalog, seek clarification from one of these offices.

Review the material in the section of this guide entitled Questions to Ask About a College's CLEP Policy. Use these guidelines to evaluate the college's CLEP policy. If you have not yet taken a CLEP examination, this evaluation will help you decide which examinations to take and whether or not to take the free-response or essay portion. Because individual colleges have different CLEP policies, a review of several policies may help you decide which college to attend.

STEP 4. If you have not yet applied for admission, do so early.

Most colleges expect you to apply for admission several months before you enroll, and it is essential that you meet the published application deadlines. It takes time to process your application for admission; and if you have yet to take a CLEP examination, it will be some time before the college receives and reviews your score report. You will probably want to take some, if not all, of the CLEP examinations you are interested in before you enroll so you know which courses you need not register for. In fact, some colleges require that all CLEP scores be submitted before a student registers.

Complete all forms and include all documents requested with your application(s) for admission. Normally, an admissions decision cannot be reached until all documents have been submitted and evaluated. Unless told to do so, do not send your CLEP scores until you have been officially admitted.

STEP 5. Arrange to take CLEP examination(s) or to submit your CLEP score(s).

You may want to wait to take your CLEP examinations until you know definitely which college you will be attending. Then you can make sure you are taking tests your college will accept for credit. You will also be able to request that your scores be sent to the college, free of charge, when you take the tests.

If you have already taken CLEP examinations, but did not have a copy of your score report sent to your college, you may request the College Board to send an official transcript at any time for a small fee. Use the Transcript Request Form that was sent to you with your score report. If you do not have the form, you may find it online at www.collegeboard.com/clep.

Your CLEP scores will be evaluated, probably by someone in the admissions office, and sent to the registrar's office to be posted on your permanent record once you are enrolled. Procedures vary from college to college, but the process usually begins in the admissions office.

STEP 6. Ask to receive a written notice of the credit you receive for your CLEP score(s).

A written notice may save you problems later, when you submit your degree plan or file for graduation. In the event that there is a question about whether or not you earned CLEP credit, you will have an official record of what credit was awarded. You may also need this verification of course credit if you go for academic counseling before the credit is posted on your permanent record.

STEP 7. Before you register for courses, seek academic counseling.

A discussion with your academic advisor can prevent you from taking unnecessary courses and can tell you specifically what your CLEP credit will mean to you. This step may be accomplished at the time you enroll. Most colleges have orientation sessions for new students prior to each enrollment period. During orientation, students are usually assigned an academic advisor who then gives them individual help in developing long-range plans and a course schedule for the next semester. In conjunction with this counseling, you may be asked to take some additional tests so that you can be placed at the proper course level.

External Degree Programs

If you have acquired a considerable amount of college-level knowledge through job experience, reading, or noncredit courses, if you have accumulated college credits at a variety of colleges over a period of years, or if you prefer studying on your own rather than in a classroom setting, you may want to investigate the possibility of enrolling in an external degree program. Many colleges offer external degree programs that allow you to earn a degree by passing examinations (including CLEP), transferring credit from other colleges, and demonstrating in other ways that you have satisfied the educational requirements. No classroom attendance is required, and the programs are open to out-of-state candidates as well as residents. Thomas A. Edison State College in New Jersey and Charter Oaks College in Connecticut are fully accredited independent state colleges; the New York program is part of the state university system and is also fully accredited. If you are interested in exploring an external degree, you can write for more information to:

Charter Oak College
The Exchange, Suite 171
270 Farmington Avenue
Farmington, CT 06032-1909

Regents External Degree Program
Cultural Education Center
Empire State Plaza
Albany, New York 12230

Thomas A. Edison State College
101 West State Street
Trenton, New Jersey 08608

Many other colleges also have external degree or weekend programs. While they often require that a number of courses be taken on campus, the external degree programs tend to be more flexible in transferring credit, granting credit-by-examination, and allowing independent study than other traditional programs. When applying to a college, you may wish to ask whether it has an external degree or weekend program.

Questions to Ask About a College's CLEP Policy

Before taking CLEP examinations for the purpose of earning college credit, try to find the answers to these questions:

1. Which CLEP examinations are accepted by this college?

A college may accept some CLEP examinations for credit and not others - possibly not the one you are considering. The English faculty may decide to grant college English credit based on the CLEP English Composition examination, but not on the Freshman College Composition examination. Or, the mathematics faculty may decide to grant credit based on the College Mathematics to non-mathematics majors only, requiring majors to take an examination in algebra, trigonometry, or calculus to earn credit. For these reasons, it is important that you know the specific CLEP tests for which you can receive credit.

2. Does the college require the optional free-response (essay) section as well as the objective portion of the CLEP examination you are considering?

Knowing the answer to this question ahead of time will permit you to schedule the optional essay examination when you register to take your CLEP examination.

3. Is credit granted for specific courses? If so, which ones?

You are likely to find that credit will be granted for specific courses and the course titles will be designated in the college's CLEP policy. It is not necessary, however, that credit be granted for a specific course in order for you to benefit from your CLEP credit. For instance, at many liberal arts colleges, all students must take certain types of courses; these courses may be labeled the core curriculum, general education requirements, distribution requirements, or liberal arts requirements. The requirements are often expressed in terms of credit hours. For example, all students may be required to take at least six hours of humanities, six hours of English, three hours of mathematics, six hours of natural science, and six hours of social science, with no particular courses in these disciplines specified. In these instances, CLEP credit may be given as 6 hrs. English credit or 3 hrs. Math credit without specifying for which English or mathematics courses credit has been awarded. In order to avoid possible disappointment, you should know before taking a CLEP examination what type of credit you can receive and whether you will only be exempted from a required course but receive no credit.

4. How much credit is granted for each examination you are considering, and does the college place a limit on the total amount of CLEP credit you can earn toward your degree?

Not all colleges that grant CLEP credit award the same amount for individual tests. Furthermore, some colleges place a limit on the total amount of credit you can earn through CLEP or other examinations. Other colleges may grant you exemption but no credit toward your degree. Knowing several colleges' policies concerning these issues may help you decide which college you will attend. If you think you are capable of passing a number of CLEP examinations, you may want to attend a college that will allow you to earn credit for all or most of them. For example, the state external degree programs grant credit for most CLEP examinations (and other tests as well).

5. What is the required score for earning CLEP credit for each test you are considering?

Most colleges publish the required scores or percentile ranks for earning CLEP credit in their general catalog or in a brochure. The required score may vary from test to test, so find out the required score for each test you are considering.

6. What is the college's policy regarding prior course work in the subject in which you are considering taking a CLEP test?

Some colleges will not grant credit for a CLEP test if the student has already attempted a college-level course closely aligned with that test. For example, if you successfully completed English 101 or a comparable course on another campus, you will probably not be permitted to receive CLEP credit in that subject, too. Some colleges will not permit you to earn CLEP credit for a course that you failed.

7. Does the college make additional stipulations before credit will be granted?

It is common practice for colleges to award CLEP credit only to their enrolled students. There are other stipulations, however, that vary from college to college. For example, does the college require you to formally apply for or accept CLEP credit by completing and signing a form? Or does the college require you to validate your CLEP score by successfully completing a more advanced course in the subject? Answers to these and other questions will help to smooth the process of earning college credit through CLEP.

The above questions and the discussions that follow them indicate some of the ways in which colleges' CLEP policies can vary. Find out as much as possible about the CLEP policies at the colleges you are interested in so you can choose a college with a policy that is compatible with your educational goals. Once you have selected the college you will attend, you can find out which CLEP examinations your college recognizes and the requirements for earning CLEP credit.

DECIDING WHICH EXAMINATIONS TO TAKE

If You're Taking the Examinations for College Credit or Career Advancement:

Most people who take CLEP examinations do so in order to earn credit for college courses. Others take the examinations in order to qualify for job promotions or for professional certification or licensing. It is vital to most candidates who are taking the tests for any of these reasons that they be well prepared for the tests they are taking so that they can advance as rapidly as possible toward their educational or career goals.

It is usually advisable that those who have limited knowledge in the subjects covered by the tests they are considering enroll in the college courses in which that material is taught. Those who are uncertain about whether or not they know enough about a subject to do well on a particular CLEP test will find the following guidelines helpful.

There is no way to predict if you will pass a particular CLEP examination, but answers to the questions under the seven headings below should give you an indication of whether or not you are likely to succeed.

1. Test Descriptions

Read the description of the test provided. Are you familiar with most of the topics and terminology in the outline?

2. Textbooks

Examine the suggested textbooks and other resource materials following the test descriptions in this guide. Have you recently read one or more of these books, or have you read similar college-level books on this subject? If you have not, read through one or more of the textbooks listed, or through the textbook used for this course at your college. Are you familiar with most of the topics and terminology in the book?

3. Sample Questions

The sample questions provided are intended to be typical of the content and difficulty of the questions on the test. Although they are not an exact miniature of the test, the proportion of the sample questions you can answer correctly should be a rough estimate of the proportion of questions you will be able to answer correctly on the test.

Answer as many of the sample questions for this test as you can. Check your answers against the correct answers. Did you answer more than half the questions correctly?

Because of variations in course content at different institutions, and because questions on CLEP tests vary from easy to difficult - with most being of moderate difficulty - the average student who passes a course in a subject can usually answer correctly about half the questions on the corresponding CLEP examination. Most colleges set their passing scores near this level, but some set them higher. If your college has set its required score above the level required by most colleges, you may need to answer a larger proportion of questions on the test correctly.

4. Previous Study

Have you taken noncredit courses in this subject offered by an adult school or a private school, through correspondence, or in connection with your job? Did you do exceptionally well in this subject in high school, or did you take an honors course in this subject?

5. Experience

Have you learned or used the knowledge or skills included in this test in your job or life experience? For example, if you lived in a Spanish-speaking country and spoke the language for a year or more, you might consider taking the Spanish examination. Or, if you have worked at a job in which you used accounting and finance skills, Principles of Accounting would be a likely test for you to take. Or, if you have read a considerable amount of literature and attended many art exhibits, concerts, and plays, you might expect to do well on the Humanities exam.

6. Other Examinations

Have you done well on other standardized tests in subjects related to the one you want to take? For example, did you score well above average on a portion of a college entrance examination covering similar skills, or did you obtain an exceptionally high score on a high school equivalency test or a licensing examination in this subject? Although such tests do not cover exactly the same material as the CLEP examinations and may be easier, persons who do well on these tests often do well on CLEP examinations, too.

7. Advice

Has a college counselor, professor, or some other professional person familiar with your ability advised you to take a CLEP examination?

If your answer was yes to questions under several of the above headings, you probably have a good chance of passing the CLEP examination you are considering. It is unlikely that you would have acquired sufficient background from experience alone. Learning gained through reading and study is essential, and you will probably find some additional study helpful before taking a CLEP examination.

If You're Taking the Examinations to Prepare for College

Many people entering college, particularly adults returning to college after several years away from formal education, are uncertain about their ability to compete with other college students. They wonder whether they have sufficient background for college study, and those who have been away from formal study for some time wonder whether they have forgotten how to study, how to take tests, and how to write papers. Such people may wish to improve their test-taking and study skills prior to enrolling in courses.

One way to assess your ability to perform at the college level and to improve your test-taking and study skills at the same time is to prepare for and take one or more CLEP examinations. You need not be enrolled in a college to take a CLEP examination, and you may have your scores sent only to yourself and later request that a transcript be sent to a college if you then decide to apply for credit. By reviewing the test descriptions and sample questions, you may find one or several subject areas in which you think you have substantial knowledge. Select one examination, or more if you like, and carefully read at least one of the textbooks listed in the bibliography for the test. By doing this, you will get a better idea of how much you know of what is usually taught in a college-level course in that subject. Study as much material as you can, until you think you have a good grasp of the subject matter. Then take the test at a college in your area. It will be several weeks before you receive your results, and you may wish to begin reviewing for another test in the meantime.

To find out if you are eligible for credit for your CLEP score, you must compare your score with the score required by the college you plan to attend. If you are not yet sure which college you will attend, or whether you will enroll in college at all, you should begin to follow the steps outlined. It is best that you do this before taking a CLEP test, but if you are taking the test only for the experience and to familiarize yourself with college-level material and requirements, you might take the test before you approach a college. Even if the college you decide to attend does not accept the test you took, the experience of taking such a test will enable you to meet with greater confidence the requirements of courses you will take.

You will find information about how to interpret your scores in WHAT YOUR SCORES MEAN, which you will receive with your score report, and which can also be found online at the CLEP website. Many colleges follow the recommendations of the American Council on Education (ACE) for setting their required scores, so you can use this information as a guide in determining how well you did. The ACE recommendations are included in the booklet.

If you do not do well enough on the test to earn college credit, don't be discouraged. Usually, it is the best college students who are exempted from courses or receive credit-by-examination. The fact that you cannot get credit for your score means that you should probably enroll in a college course to learn the material. However, if your score was close to the required score, or if you feel you could do better on a second try or after some additional study, you may retake the test after six months. Do not take it sooner or your score will not be reported and your fee will be forfeited.

If you do earn the score required to earn credit, you will have demonstrated that you already have some college-level knowledge. You will also have a better idea whether you should take additional CLEP examinations. And, what is most important, you can enroll in college with confidence, knowing that you do have the ability to succeed.

PREPARING TO TAKE CLEP EXAMINATIONS

Having made the decision to take one or more CLEP examinations, most people then want to know if it is worthwhile to prepare for them - how much, how long, when, and how should they go about it? The precise answers to these questions vary greatly from individual to individual. However, most candidates find that some type of test preparation is helpful.

Most people who take CLEP examinations do so to show that they have already learned the important material that is taught in a college course. Many of them need only a quick review to assure themselves that they have not forgotten some of what they once studied, and to fill in some of the gaps in their knowledge of the subject. Others feel that they need a thorough review and spend several weeks studying for a test. A few wish to take a CLEP examination as a kind of final examination for independent study of a subject instead of the college course. This last group requires significantly more study than those who only need to review, and they may need some guidance from professors of the subjects they are studying.

The key to how you prepare for CLEP examinations often lies in locating those skills and areas of prior learning in which you are strong and deciding where to focus your energies. Some people may know a great deal about a certain subject area, but may not test well. These individuals would probably be just as concerned about strengthening their test-taking skills as they are about studying for a specific test. Many mental and physical skills are used in preparing for a test. It is important not only to review or study for the examinations, but to make certain that you are alert, relatively free of anxiety, and aware of how to approach standardized tests. Suggestions on developing test-taking skills and preparing psychologically and physically for a test are given. The following section suggests ways of assessing your knowledge of the content of a test and then reviewing and studying the material.

Using This Study Guide

Begin by carefully reading the test description and outline of knowledge and skills required for the examination, if given. As you read through the topics listed there, ask yourself how much you know about each one. Also note the terms, names, and symbols that are mentioned, and ask yourself whether you are familiar with them. This will give you a quick overview of how much you know about the subject. If you are familiar with nearly all the material, you will probably need a minimum of review; however, if less than half of it is familiar, you will probably require substantial study to do well on the test.

If, after reviewing the test description, you find that you need extensive review, delay answering the sample question until you have done some reading in the subject. If you complete them before reviewing the material, you will probably look for the answers as you study, and then they will not be a good assessment of your ability at a later date.

If you think you are familiar with most of the test material, try to answer the sample questions.

Apply the test-taking strategies given. Keeping within the time limit suggested will give you a rough idea of how quickly you should work in order to complete the actual test.

Check your answers against the answer key. If you answered nearly all the questions correctly, you probably do not need to study the subject extensively. If you got about half the questions correct, you ought o review at least one textbook or other suggested materials on the subject. If you answered less than half the questions correctly, you will probably benefit from more extensive reading in the subject and thorough study of one or more textbooks. The textbooks listed are used at many colleges but they are not the only good texts. You will find helpful almost any standard text available to you., such as the textbook used at your college, or earlier editions of texts listed. For some examinations, topic outlines and textbooks may not be available. Take the sample tests in this book and check your answers at the end of each test. Check wrong answers.

Suggestions for Studying

The following suggestions have been gathered from people who have prepared for CLEP examinations or other college-level tests.

1. Define your goals and locate study materials

First, determine your study goals. Set aside a block of time to review the material provided in this book, and then decide which test(s) you will take. Using the suggestions, locate suitable resource materials. If a preparation course is offered by an adult school or college in your area, you might find it helpful to enroll.

2. Find a good place to study

To determine what kind of place you need for studying, ask yourself questions such as: Do I need a quiet place? Does the telephone distract me? Do objects I see in this place remind me of things I should do? Is it too warm? Is it well lit? Am I too comfortable here? Do I have space to spread out my materials? You may find the library more conducive to studying than your home. If you decide to study at home, you might prevent interruptions by other household members by putting a sign on the door of your study room to indicate when you will be available.

3. Schedule time to study

To help you determine where studying best fits into your schedule, try this exercise: Make a list of your daily activities (for example, sleeping, working, and eating) and estimate how many hours per day you spend on each activity. Now, rate all the activities on your list in order of their importance and evaluate your use of time. Often people are astonished at how an average day appears from this perspective. They may discover that they were unaware how large portions of time are spent, or they learn their time can be scheduled in alternative ways. For example, they can remove the least important activities from their day and devote that time to studying or another important activity.

4. Establish a study routine and a set of goals

In order to study effectively, you should establish specific goals and a schedule for accomplishing them. Some people find it helpful to write out a weekly schedule and cross out each study period when it is completed. Others maintain their concentration better by writing down the time when they expect to complete a study task. Most people find short periods of intense study more productive than long stretches of time. For example, they may follow a regular schedule of several 20- or 30-minute study periods with short breaks between them. Some people like to allow themselves rewards as they complete each study goal. It is not essential that you accomplish every goal exactly within your schedule; the point is to be committed to your task.

5. Learn how to take an active role in studying.

If you have not done much studying for some time, you may find it difficult to concentrate at first. Try a method of studying, such as the one outlined below, that will help you concentrate on and remember what you read.

    a. First, read the chapter summary and the introduction. Then you will know what to look for in your reading.

    b. Next, convert the section or paragraph headlines into questions. For example, if you are reading a section entitled, The Causes of the American Revolution, ask yourself: *What were the causes of the American Revolution?* Compose the answer as you read the paragraph. Reading and answering questions aloud will help you understand and remember the material.

c. Take notes on key ideas or concepts as you read. Writing will also help you fix concepts more firmly in your mind. Underlining key ideas or writing notes in your book can be helpful and will be useful for review. Underline only important points. If you underline more than a third of each paragraph, you are probably underlining too much.

d. If there are questions or problems at the end of a chapter, answer or solve them on paper as if you were asked to do them for homework. Mathematics textbooks (and some other books) sometimes include answers to some or all of the exercises. If you have such a book, write your answers before looking at the ones given. When problem-solving is involved, work enough problems to master the required methods and concepts. If you have difficulty with problems, review any sample problems or explanations in the chapter.

e. To retain knowledge, most people have to review the material periodically. If you are preparing for a test over an extended period of time, review key concepts and notes each week or so. Do not wait for weeks to review the material or you will need to relearn much of it.

Psychological and Physical Preparation

Most people feel at least some nervousness before taking a test. Adults who are returning to college may not have taken a test in many years or they may have had little experience with standardized tests. Some younger students, as well, are uncomfortable with testing situations. People who received their education in countries outside the United States may find that many tests given in this country are quite different from the ones they are accustomed to taking.

Not only might candidates find the types of tests and the kinds of questions on them unfamiliar, but other aspects of the testing environment may be strange as well. The physical and mental stress that results from meeting this new experience can hinder a candidate's ability to demonstrate his or her true degree of knowledge in the subject area being tested. For this reason, it is important to go to the test center well prepared, both mentally and physically, for taking the test. You may find the following suggestions helpful.

1. Familiarize yourself, as much as possible, with the test and the test situation before the day of the examination. It will be helpful for you to know ahead of time:

a. How much time will be allowed for the test and whether there are timed subsections.

b. What types of questions and directions appear on the examination.

c. How your test score will be computed.

d. How to properly answer the questions on the computer (See the CLEP Sample on the CLEP website)

e. In which building and room the examination will be administered. If you don't know where the building is, locate it or get directions ahead of time.

f. The time of the test administration. You might wish to confirm this information a day or two before the examination and find out what time the building and room will be open so that you can plan to arrive early.

g. Where to park your car or, if you wish to take public transportation, which bus or train to take and the location of the nearest stop.

h. Whether smoking will be permitted during the test.

i. Whether there will be a break between examinations (if you will be taking more than one on the same day), and whether there is a place nearby where you can get something to eat or drink.

2. Go to the test situation relaxed and alert. In order to prepare for the test:

a. Get a good night's sleep. Last minute cramming, particularly late the night before, is usually counterproductive.

b. Eat normally. It is usually not wise to skip breakfast or lunch on the day of the test or to eat a big meal just before the test.

c. Avoid tranquilizers and stimulants. If you follow the other directions in this book, you won't need artificial aids. It's better to be a little tense than to be drowsy, but stimulants such as coffee and cola can make you nervous and interfere with your concentration.

d. Don't drink a lot of liquids before the test. Having to leave the room during the test will disturb your concentration and take valuable time away from the test.

e. If you are inclined to be nervous or tense, learn some relaxation exercises and use them before and perhaps during the test.

3. Arrive for the test early and prepared. Be sure to:

a. Arrive early enough so that you can find a parking place, locate the test center, and get settled comfortably before testing begins. Allow some extra time in case you are delayed unexpectedly.

b. Take the following with you:

- Your completed Registration/Admission Form
- Two forms of identification – one being a government-issued photo ID with signature, such as a driver's license or passport
- Non-mechanical pencil
- A watch so that you can time your progress (digital watches are prohibited)
- Your glasses if you need them for reading or seeing the chalkboard or wall clock

c. Leave all books, papers, and notes outside the test center. You will not be permitted to use your own scratch paper; it will be provided. Also prohibited are calculators, cell phones, beepers, pagers, photo/copy devices, radios, headphones, food, beverages, and several other items.

d. Be prepared for any temperature in the testing room. Wear layers of clothing that can be removed if the room is too hot but will keep you warm if it is too cold.

4. When you enter the test room:

a. Sit in a seat that provides a maximum of comfort and freedom from distraction.

b. Read directions carefully, and listen to all instructions given by the test administrator. If you don't understand the directions, ask for help before test timing begins. If you must ask a question after the test has begun, raise your hand and a proctor will assist you. The proctor can answer certain kinds of questions but cannot help you with the test.

c. Know your rights as a test taker. You can expect to be given the full working time allowed for the test(s) and a reasonably quiet and comfortable place in which to work. If a poor test situation is preventing you from doing your best, ask if the situation can be remedied. If bad test conditions cannot be remedied, ask the person in charge to report the problem in the Irregularity Report that will be sent to ETS with the answer sheets. You may also wish to contact CLEP. Describe the exact circumstances as completely as you can. Be sure to include the test date and name(s) of the test(s) you took. ETS will investigate the problem to make sure it does not happen again, and, if the problem is serious enough, may arrange for you to retake the test without charge.

TAKING THE EXAMINATIONS

A person may know a great deal about the subject being tested, but not do as well as he or she is capable of on the test. Knowing how to approach a test is an important part of the testing process. While a command of test-taking skills cannot substitute for knowledge of the subject matter, it can be a significant factor in successful testing.

Test-taking skills enable a person to use all available information to earn a score that truly reflects his or her ability. There are different strategies for approaching different kinds of test questions. For example, free-response questions require a very different tack than do multiple-choice questions. Other factors, such as how the test will be graded, may also influence your approach to the test and your use of test time. Thus, your preparation for a test should include finding out all you can about the test so that you can use the most effective test-taking strategies.

Before taking a test, you should know approximately how many questions are on the test, how much time you will be allowed, how the test will be scored or graded, what types of questions and directions are on the test, and how you will be required to record your answers.

Taking Multiple-Choice Tests

1. Listen carefully to the instructions given by the test administrator and read carefully all directions before you begin to answer the questions.

2. Note the time that the test administrator starts timing the test. As you proceed, make sure that you are not working too slowly. You should have answered at least half the questions in a section when half the time for that section has passed. If you have not reached that point in the section, speed up your pace on the remaining questions.

3. Before answering a question, read the entire question, including all the answer choices. Don't think that because the first or second answer choice looks good to you, it isn't necessary to read the remaining options. Instructions usually tell you to select the best answer. Sometimes one answer choice is partially correct, but another option is better; therefore, it is usually a good idea to read all the answers before you choose one.

4. Read and consider every question. Questions that look complicated at first glance may not actually be so difficult once you have read them carefully.

5. Do not puzzle too long over any one question. If you don't know the answer after you've considered it briefly, go on to the next question. Make sure you return to the question later.

6. Make sure you record your response properly.

7. In trying to determine the correct answer, you may find it helpful to cross out those options that you know are incorrect, and to make marks next to those you think might be correct. If you decide to skip the question and come back to it later, you will save yourself the time of reconsidering all the options.

8. Watch for the following key words in test questions:

all	generally	never	perhaps
always	however	none	rarely
but	may	not	seldom
except	must	often	sometimes
every	necessary	only	usually

When a question or answer option contains words such as always, every, only, never, and none, there can be no exceptions to the answer you choose. Use of words such as often, rarely, sometimes, and generally indicates that there may be some exceptions to the answer.

9. Do not waste your time looking for clues to right answers based on flaws in question wording or patterns in correct answers. Professionals at the College Board and ETS put

a great deal of effort into developing valid, reliable, fair tests. CLEP test development committees are composed of college faculty who are experts in the subject covered by the test and are appointed by the College Board to write test questions and to scrutinize each question that is included on a CLEP test. Committee members make every effort to ensure that the questions are not ambiguous, that they have only one correct answer, and that they cover college-level topics. These committees do not intentionally include trick questions. If you think a question is flawed, ask the test administrator to report it, or contact CLEP immediately.

Taking Free-Response or Essay Tests

If your college requires the optional free-response or essay portion of a CLEP Composition and Literature exams, you should do some additional preparation for your CLEP test. Taking an essay test is very different from taking a multiple-choice test, so you will need to use some other strategies.

The essay written as part of the English Composition and Essay exam is graded by English professors from a variety of colleges and universities. A process called holistic scoring is used to rate your writing ability.

The optional free-response essays, on the other hand, are graded by the faculty of the college you designate as a score recipient. Guidelines and criteria for grading essays are not specified by the College Board or ETS. You may find it helpful, therefore, to talk with someone at your college to find out what criteria will be used to determine whether you will get credit. If the test requires essay responses, ask how much emphasis will be placed on your writing ability and your ability to organize your thoughts as opposed to your knowledge of subject matter. Find out how much weight will be given to your multiple-choice test score in comparison with your free-response grade in determining whether you will get credit. This will give you an idea where you should expend the greatest effort in preparing for and taking the test.

Here are some strategies you will find useful in taking any essay test:

1. Before you begin to write, read all questions carefully and take a few minutes to jot down some ideas you might include in each answer.

2. If you are given a choice of questions to answer, choose the questions you think you can answer most clearly and knowledgeably.

3. Determine in what order you will answer the questions. Answer those you find the easiest first so that any extra time can be spent on the more difficult questions.

4. When you know which questions you will answer and in what order, determine how much testing time remains and estimate how many minutes you will devote to each question. Unless suggested times are given for the questions or one question appears to require more or less time than the others, allot an equal amount of time to each question.

5. Before answering each question, indicate the number of the question as it is given in the test book. You need not copy the entire question from the question sheet, but it will be helpful to you and to the person grading your test if you indicate briefly the topic you are addressing – particularly if you are not answering the questions in the order in which they appear on the test.

6. Before answering each question, read it again carefully to make sure you are interpreting it correctly. Underline key words, such as those listed below, that often appear in free-response questions. Be sure you know the exact meaning of these words before taking the test.

analyze	demonstrate	enumerate	list
apply	derive	explain	outline
assess	describe	generalize	prove
compare	determine	illustrate	rank
contrast	discuss	interpret	show
define	distinguish	justify	summarize

If a question asks you to outline, define, or summarize, do not write a detailed explanation; if a question asks you to analyze, explain, illustrate, interpret, or show, you must do more than briefly describe the topic.

For a current listing of CLEP Colleges

where you can get credit and be tested, write:

CLEP, P.O. Box 6600, Princeton, NJ 08541-6600

Or e-mail: clep@ets.org, or call: (609) 771-7865

Principles of Marketing

Description of the Examination
The Principles of Marketing examination covers the material that is usually taught in a one-semester introductory course in marketing. Such a course is usually known as Basic Marketing, Introduction to Marketing, Fundamentals of Marketing, Marketing, or Marketing Principles. The exam is concerned with the role of marketing in society and within a firm, understanding consumer and organizational markets, marketing strategy planning, the marketing mix, marketing institutions, and other selected topics, such as international marketing, ethics, marketing research, services and not-for-profit marketing. The candidate is also expected to have a basic knowledge of the economic/demographic, social/cultural, political/legal, and technological trends that are important to marketing.

The examination contains approximately 100 questions to be answered in 90 minutes. Some of these are pretest questions that will not be scored. Any time candidates spend on tutorials and providing personal information is in addition to the actual testing time.

Knowledge and Skills Required
The subject matter of the Principles of Marketing examination is drawn from the following topics in the approximate proportions indicated. The percentages next to the main topics indicate the approximate percentage of exam questions on that topic.

8-13% Role of Marketing in Society
- Ethics
- Nonprofit marketing
- International marketing

17-24% Role of Marketing in a Firm
- Marketing concept
- Marketing strategy
- Marketing environment
- Marketing decision system
    - Marketing research
    - Marketing information system

22-27% Target Marketing
- Consumer behavior
- Segmentation
- Positioning
- Business-to-business markets

40-50% Marketing Mix
- Product and service management
- Branding
- Pricing policies
- Distribution channels and logistics
- Integrated marketing communications/Promotion
- Marketing application in e-commerce

HOW TO TAKE A TEST

You have studied long, hard and conscientiously.

With your official admission card in hand, and your heart pounding, you have been admitted to the examination room.

You note that there are several hundred other applicants in the examination room waiting to take the same test.

They all appear to be equally well prepared.

You know that nothing but your best effort will suffice. The "moment of truth" is at hand: you now have to demonstrate objectively, in writing, your knowledge of content and your understanding of subject matter.

You are fighting the most important battle of your life—to pass and/or score high on an examination which will determine your career and provide the economic basis for your livelihood.

What extra, special things should you know and should you do in taking the examination?

I. YOU MUST PASS AN EXAMINATION

A. WHAT EVERY CANDIDATE SHOULD KNOW
Examination applicants often ask us for help in preparing for the written test. What can I study in advance? What kinds of questions will be asked? How will the test be given? How will the papers be graded?

B. HOW ARE EXAMS DEVELOPED?
Examinations are carefully written by trained technicians who are specialists in the field known as "psychological measurement," in consultation with recognized authorities in the field of work that the test will cover. These experts recommend the subject matter areas or skills to be tested; only those knowledges or skills important to your success on the job are included. The most reliable books and source materials available are used as references. Together, the experts and technicians judge the difficulty level of the questions.
Test technicians know how to phrase questions so that the problem is clearly stated. Their ethics do not permit "trick" or "catch" questions. Questions may have been tried out on sample groups, or subjected to statistical analysis, to determine their usefulness.
Written tests are often used in combination with performance tests, ratings of training and experience, and oral interviews. All of these measures combine to form the best-known means of finding the right person for the right job.

II. HOW TO PASS THE WRITTEN TEST

A. BASIC STEPS

1) Study the announcement

How, then, can you know what subjects to study? Our best answer is: "Learn as much as possible about the class of positions for which you've applied." The exam will test the knowledge, skills and abilities needed to do the work.

Your most valuable source of information about the position you want is the official exam announcement. This announcement lists the training and experience qualifications. Check these standards and apply only if you come reasonably close to meeting them. Many jurisdictions preview the written test in the exam announcement by including a section called "Knowledge and Abilities Required," "Scope of the Examination," or some similar heading. Here you will find out specifically what fields will be tested.

2) Choose appropriate study materials

If the position for which you are applying is technical or advanced, you will read more advanced, specialized material. If you are already familiar with the basic principles of your field, elementary textbooks would waste your time. Concentrate on advanced textbooks and technical periodicals. Think through the concepts and review difficult problems in your field.

These are all general sources. You can get more ideas on your own initiative, following these leads. For example, training manuals and publications of the government agency which employs workers in your field can be useful, particularly for technical and professional positions. A letter or visit to the government department involved may result in more specific study suggestions, and certainly will provide you with a more definite idea of the exact nature of the position you are seeking.

3) Study this book!

III. KINDS OF TESTS

Tests are used for purposes other than measuring knowledge and ability to perform specified duties. For some positions, it is equally important to test ability to make adjustments to new situations or to profit from training. In others, basic mental abilities not dependent on information are essential. Questions which test these things may not appear as pertinent to the duties of the position as those which test for knowledge and information. Yet they are often highly important parts of a fair examination. For very general questions, it is almost impossible to help you direct your study efforts. What we can do is to point out some of the more common of these general abilities needed in public service positions and describe some typical questions.

1) General information

Broad, general information has been found useful for predicting job success in some kinds of work. This is tested in a variety of ways, from vocabulary lists to questions about current events. Basic background in some field of work, such as sociology or economics, may be sampled in a group of questions. Often these are principles which have become familiar to most persons through exposure rather than through formal training. It is difficult to advise you how to study for these questions; being alert to the world around you is our best suggestion.

2) Verbal ability

An example of an ability needed in many positions is verbal or language ability. Verbal ability is, in brief, the ability to use and understand words. Vocabulary and grammar tests are typical measures of this ability. Reading comprehension or paragraph interpretation questions are common in many kinds of civil service tests. You are given a paragraph of written material and asked to find its central meaning.

IV. KINDS OF QUESTIONS

1. Multiple-choice Questions

Most popular of the short-answer questions is the "multiple choice" or "best answer" question. It can be used, for example, to test for factual knowledge, ability to solve problems or judgment in meeting situations found at work.

A multiple-choice question is normally one of three types:
- It can begin with an incomplete statement followed by several possible endings. You are to find the one ending which best completes the statement, although some of the others may not be entirely wrong.
- It can also be a complete statement in the form of a question which is answered by choosing one of the statements listed.
- It can be in the form of a problem – again you select the best answer.

Here is an example of a multiple-choice question with a discussion which should give you some clues as to the method for choosing the right answer:

When an employee has a complaint about his assignment, the action which will best help him overcome his difficulty is to
    A. discuss his difficulty with his coworkers
    B. take the problem to the head of the organization
    C. take the problem to the person who gave him the assignment
    D. say nothing to anyone about his complaint

In answering this question, you should study each of the choices to find which is best. Consider choice "A" – Certainly an employee may discuss his complaint with fellow employees, but no change or improvement can result, and the complaint remains unresolved. Choice "B" is a poor choice since the head of the organization probably does not know what assignment you have been given, and taking your problem to him is known as "going over the head" of the supervisor. The supervisor, or person who made the assignment, is the person who can clarify it or correct any injustice. Choice "C" is, therefore, correct. To say nothing, as in choice "D," is unwise. Supervisors have and interest in knowing the problems employees are facing, and the employee is seeking a solution to his problem.

2. True/False

3. Matching Questions
Matching an answer from a column of choices within another column.

V. RECORDING YOUR ANSWERS

Computer terminals are used more and more today for many different kinds of exams.

For an examination with very few applicants, you may be told to record your answers in the test booklet itself. Separate answer sheets are much more common. If this separate answer sheet is to be scored by machine – and this is often the case – it is highly important that you mark your answers correctly in order to get credit.

VI. BEFORE THE TEST

YOUR PHYSICAL CONDITION IS IMPORTANT

If you are not well, you can't do your best work on tests. If you are half asleep, you can't do your best either. Here are some tips:

1) Get about the same amount of sleep you usually get. Don't stay up all night before the test, either partying or worrying—DON'T DO IT!
2) If you wear glasses, be sure to wear them when you go to take the test. This goes for hearing aids, too.
3) If you have any physical problems that may keep you from doing your best, be sure to tell the person giving the test. If you are sick or in poor health, you relay cannot do your best on any test. You can always come back and take the test some other time.

Common sense will help you find procedures to follow to get ready for an examination. Too many of us, however, overlook these sensible measures. Indeed, nervousness and fatigue have been found to be the most serious reasons why applicants fail to do their best on civil service tests. Here is a list of reminders:

- Begin your preparation early – Don't wait until the last minute to go scurrying around for books and materials or to find out what the position is all about.
- Prepare continuously – An hour a night for a week is better than an all-night cram session. This has been definitely established. What is more, a night a week for a month will return better dividends than crowding your study into a shorter period of time.
- Locate the place of the exam – You have been sent a notice telling you when and where to report for the examination. If the location is in a different town or otherwise unfamiliar to you, it would be well to inquire the best route and learn something about the building.
- Relax the night before the test – Allow your mind to rest. Do not study at all that night. Plan some mild recreation or diversion; then go to bed early and get a good night's sleep.
- Get up early enough to make a leisurely trip to the place for the test – This way unforeseen events, traffic snarls, unfamiliar buildings, etc. will not upset you.
- Dress comfortably – A written test is not a fashion show. You will be known by number and not by name, so wear something comfortable.
- Leave excess paraphernalia at home – Shopping bags and odd bundles will get in your way. You need bring only the items mentioned in the official notice you received; usually everything you need is provided. Do not bring reference books to the exam. They will only confuse those last minutes and be taken away from you when in the test room.

- Arrive somewhat ahead of time – If because of transportation schedules you must get there very early, bring a newspaper or magazine to take your mind off yourself while waiting.
- Locate the examination room – When you have found the proper room, you will be directed to the seat or part of the room where you will sit. Sometimes you are given a sheet of instructions to read while you are waiting. Do not fill out any forms until you are told to do so; just read them and be prepared.
- Relax and prepare to listen to the instructions
- If you have any physical problem that may keep you from doing your best, be sure to tell the test administrator. If you are sick or in poor health, you really cannot do your best on the exam. You can come back and take the test some other time.

VII. AT THE TEST

The day of the test is here and you have the test booklet in your hand. The temptation to get going is very strong. Caution! There is more to success than knowing the right answers. You must know how to identify your papers and understand variations in the type of short-answer question used in this particular examination. Follow these suggestions for maximum results from your efforts:

1) Cooperate with the monitor
The test administrator has a duty to create a situation in which you can be as much at ease as possible. He will give instructions, tell you when to begin, check to see that you are marking your answer sheet correctly, and so on. He is not there to guard you, although he will see that your competitors do not take unfair advantage. He wants to help you do your best.

2) Listen to all instructions
Don't jump the gun! Wait until you understand all directions. In most civil service tests you get more time than you need to answer the questions. So don't be in a hurry. Read each word of instructions until you clearly understand the meaning. Study the examples, listen to all announcements and follow directions. Ask questions if you do not understand what to do.

3) Identify your papers
Civil service exams are usually identified by number only. You will be assigned a number; you must not put your name on your test papers. Be sure to copy your number correctly. Since more than one exam may be given, copy your exact examination title.

4) Plan your time
Unless you are told that a test is a "speed" or "rate of work" test, speed itself is usually not important. Time enough to answer all the questions will be provided, but this does not mean that you have all day. An overall time limit has been set. Divide the total time (in minutes) by the number of questions to determine the approximate time you have for each question.

5) Do not linger over difficult questions
If you come across a difficult question, mark it with a paper clip (useful to have along) and come back to it when you have been through the booklet. One caution if you do this – be sure to skip a number on your answer sheet as well. Check often to be sure that

you have not lost your place and that you are marking in the row numbered the same as the question you are answering.

6) Read the questions

Be sure you know what the question asks! Many capable people are unsuccessful because they failed to read the questions correctly.

7) Answer all questions

Unless you have been instructed that a penalty will be deducted for incorrect answers, it is better to guess than to omit a question.

8) Speed tests

It is often better NOT to guess on speed tests. It has been found that on timed tests people are tempted to spend the last few seconds before time is called in marking answers at random – without even reading them – in the hope of picking up a few extra points. To discourage this practice, the instructions may warn you that your score will be "corrected" for guessing. That is, a penalty will be applied. The incorrect answers will be deducted from the correct ones, or some other penalty formula will be used.

9) Review your answers

If you finish before time is called, go back to the questions you guessed or omitted to give them further thought. Review other answers if you have time.

10) Return your test materials

If you are ready to leave before others have finished or time is called, take ALL your materials to the monitor and leave quietly. Never take any test material with you. The monitor can discover whose papers are not complete, and taking a test booklet may be grounds for disqualification.

VIII. EXAMINATION TECHNIQUES

1) Read the general instructions carefully. These are usually printed on the first page of the exam booklet. As a rule, these instructions refer to the timing of the examination; the fact that you should not start work until the signal and must stop work at a signal, etc. If there are any special instructions, such as a choice of questions to be answered, make sure that you note this instruction carefully.

2) When you are ready to start work on the examination, that is as soon as the signal has been given, read the instructions to each question booklet, underline any key words or phrases, such as least, best, outline, describe and the like. In this way you will tend to answer as requested rather than discover on reviewing your paper that you listed without describing, that you selected the worst choice rather than the best choice, etc.

3) If the examination is of the objective or multiple-choice type – that is, each question will also give a series of possible answers: A, B, C or D, and you are called upon to select the best answer and write the letter next to that answer on your answer paper – it is advisable to start answering each question in turn. There may be anywhere from 50 to 100 such questions in the three or four hours allotted and you can see how much time would be taken if you read through all the questions before beginning to answer any. Furthermore, if you

come across a question or group of questions which you know would be difficult to answer, it would undoubtedly affect your handling of all the other questions.

4) If the examination is of the essay type and contains but a few questions, it is a moot point as to whether you should read all the questions before starting to answer any one. Of course, if you are given a choice – say five out of seven and the like – then it is essential to read all the questions so you can eliminate the two that are most difficult. If, however, you are asked to answer all the questions, there may be danger in trying to answer the easiest one first because you may find that you will spend too much time on it. The best technique is to answer the first question, then proceed to the second, etc.

5) Time your answers. Before the exam begins, write down the time it started, then add the time allowed for the examination and write down the time it must be completed, then divide the time available somewhat as follows:
    - If 3-1/2 hours are allowed, that would be 210 minutes. If you have 80 objective-type questions, that would be an average of 2-1/2 minutes per question. Allow yourself no more than 2 minutes per question, or a total of 160 minutes, which will permit about 50 minutes to review.
    - If for the time allotment of 210 minutes there are 7 essay questions to answer, that would average about 30 minutes a question. Give yourself only 25 minutes per question so that you have about 35 minutes to review.

6) The most important instruction is to read each question and make sure you know what is wanted. The second most important instruction is to time yourself properly so that you answer every question. The third most important instruction is to answer every question. Guess if you have to but include something for each question. Remember that you will receive no credit for a blank and will probably receive some credit if you write something in answer to an essay question. If you guess a letter – say "B" for a multiple-choice question – you may have guessed right. If you leave a blank as an answer to a multiple-choice question, the examiners may respect your feelings but it will not add a point to your score. Some exams may penalize you for wrong answers, so in such cases only, you may not want to guess unless you have some basis for your answer.

7) Suggestions
    a. Objective-type questions
        1. Examine the question booklet for proper sequence of pages and questions
        2. Read all instructions carefully
        3. Skip any question which seems too difficult; return to it after all other questions have been answered
        4. Apportion your time properly; do not spend too much time on any single question or group of questions
        5. Note and underline key words – all, most, fewest, least, best, worst, same, opposite, etc.
        6. Pay particular attention to negatives
        7. Note unusual option, e.g., unduly long, short, complex, different or similar in content to the body of the question
        8. Observe the use of "hedging" words – probably, may, most likely, etc.

9. Make sure that your answer is put next to the same number as the question
10. Do not second-guess unless you have good reason to believe the second answer is definitely more correct
11. Cross out original answer if you decide another answer is more accurate; do not erase until you are ready to hand your paper in
12. Answer all questions; guess unless instructed otherwise
13. Leave time for review

b. Essay questions
1. Read each question carefully
2. Determine exactly what is wanted. Underline key words or phrases.
3. Decide on outline or paragraph answer
4. Include many different points and elements unless asked to develop any one or two points or elements
5. Show impartiality by giving pros and cons unless directed to select one side only
6. Make and write down any assumptions you find necessary to answer the questions
7. Watch your English, grammar, punctuation and choice of words
8. Time your answers; don't crowd material

8) Answering the essay question

Most essay questions can be answered by framing the specific response around several key words or ideas. Here are a few such key words or ideas:

M's: manpower, materials, methods, money, management
P's: purpose, program, policy, plan, procedure, practice, problems, pitfalls, personnel, public relations

a. Six basic steps in handling problems:
1. Preliminary plan and background development
2. Collect information, data and facts
3. Analyze and interpret information, data and facts
4. Analyze and develop solutions as well as make recommendations
5. Prepare report and sell recommendations
6. Install recommendations and follow up effectiveness

b. Pitfalls to avoid
1. Taking things for granted – A statement of the situation does not necessarily imply that each of the elements is necessarily true; for example, a complaint may be invalid and biased so that all that can be taken for granted is that a complaint has been registered
2. Considering only one side of a situation – Wherever possible, indicate several alternatives and then point out the reasons you selected the best one
3. Failing to indicate follow up – Whenever your answer indicates action on your part, make certain that you will take proper follow-up action to see how successful your recommendations, procedures or actions turn out to be
4. Taking too long in answering any single question – Remember to time your answers properly

EXAMINATION SECTION

EXAMINATION SECTION
TEST 1

DIRECTIONS: Each question or incomplete statement is followed by several suggested answers or completions. Select the one that BEST answers the question or completes the statement. *PRINT THE LETTER OF THE CORRECT ANSWER IN THE SPACE AT THE RIGHT.*

1. The MAIN advantage associated with a producer's use of a wholesaler's services is   1.____
    A. control of product promotion
    B. product security
    C. freedom to concentrate on production and development
    D. provision of an outside sales force

2. During the sales analysis process, a company's sales are broken down into fundamental units of   2.____
    A. dollar volume   B. transactions
    C. revenue   D. market share

3. A retailer wants to use a wholesaler that will perform purchasing and stocking functions for the outlet, and who will take back unsold products. What type of wholesaler should the retailer use?   3.____
    A. Rack jobber   B. Drop shipper
    C. Mail order   D. Truck

4. Which of the following is an example of convenience goods?   4.____
    A. Major appliance   B. Automobile
    C. Detergent   D. Clothing

5. A company decides to conduct an audit of its marketing productivity. Which of the following questions is it likely to ask?   5.____
    A. How logical are the company's objectives, given the more significant opportunities or threats and its relative resources?
    B. Can the organization handle the planning needed at the individual product/brand level?
    C. How well does the product line meet the line's objective?
    D. How profitable are each of the company's products or brands?

6. From the microeconomic point of view, the basic regulator of any free-market economic system is   6.____
    A. supply   B. demand   C. income   D. price

7. Which of the following is a type of sales promotion that is used *primarily* with newly introduced products?   7.____
    A. Premiums   B. Consumer sweepstakes
    C. Free samples   D. Sales contests

8. Compared to other characteristics involved in predicting consumer buying behavior, demographics are less

   A. reliable
   B. actionable
   C. subjective
   D. available

9. Which of the following practices is NOT specifically prohibited by the Clayton Act?

   A. Price discrimination
   B. Contracts in restraint of trade
   C. Interlocking directorates
   D. Intercorporate stockholdings

10. A retail product assortment is generally evaluated in terns of each of the following EXCEPT

    A. status
    B. margin
    C. completeness
    D. purpose

11. In general, which of the following is NOT one of the essential elements of an enforceable contract, whether written or unwritten?

    A. Consideration
    B. Transfer of goods or services
    C. Subject matter
    D. Capacity of parties

12. The most traditional marketing channel for consumer products is producer

    A. consumer →
    B. retailer → consumer
    C. wholesaler → retailer → consumer
    D. agent or broker → wholesaler → retailer → consumer

13. The primary *disadvantage* associated with personal selling is that

    A. smaller companies will not be able to justify many sales expenditures
    B. it generally costs more than media advertising for smaller companies
    C. the sales representative can communicate with only a relatively small number of potential customers
    D. smaller companies cannot manage geographic coverage of a region

14. Which of the following products, purchased by an individual consumer, is MOST likely to be selected through routine response behavior?

    A. Laundry detergent
    B. Clothing
    C. Kitchen appliance
    D. Electric drill

15. Typically, physical distribution costs will account for approximately _____% of a product's retail price.

    A. 5   B. 10   C. 20   D. 30

16. A _____ generally operates within the smallest geographical limits.   16.____

    A. broker   B. selling agent
    C. manufacturer's agent   D. commission merchant

17. Which of the following is NOT a significant reason why companies continually introduce   17.____
    new product lines sometimes in spite of their own highly successful products?

    A. Anticipation of unpredictable environmental or competitive changes
    B. High failure rates for most new products
    C. Company emphasis on investment capital
    D. A concern for long-term growth

18. Compared to industrial demand, consumer demand is NOT   18.____

    A. elastic   B. joint
    C. derived   D. more fluctuating

19. The MOST common method of evaluating sales performance is   19.____

    A. marketing audit   B. marketing cost analysis
    C. functional analysis   D. sales analysis

20. An intermediary serves a marketing channel by breaking down homogeneous stocks into   20.____
    smaller units for wholesalers and retailers. Which sorting activity is being performed by
    the intermediary?

    A. Sorting out   B. Accumulation
    C. Allocation   D. Assorting

21. The strategy of intensive distribution would MOST likely be used in the marketing of   21.____

    A. shopping goods   B. perishable goods
    C. specialized services   D. convenience goods

22. A company's potential customers are large in size, but few in number, and the company's   22.____
    promotional resources are limited. The company's personal selling objective would
    MOST likely be to

    A. develop new customers
    B. provide technical service to facilitate sales
    C. maintain customer loyalty
    D. win acceptance for new products

23. A consumer sees an advertisement in a magazine and ignores the photograph and cap-   23.____
    tion. Instead the customer directs her attention directly to the printed matter below the
    image.
    This is an example of

    A. selective retention   B. misperception
    C. selective distortion   D. selective exposure

24. For a strategic business unit, the adoption of a marketing management structure is MOST appropriate when

   A. the product management structure is not used as a training ground for top management
   B. a single product may be market to a large number of different markets where customers have very different requirements and preferences
   C. a business faces an extremely complex and uncertain environment
   D. products and markets are few and similar in nature

25. The Uniform Commercial Code (UCC) is NOT intended to

   A. shift the emphasis away from the concept of property to the concept of contract
   B. make laws uniform among various jurisdictions
   C. establish recommendations for handling warranty or product liability disputes
   D. simplify and de-emphasize the concept of title determination

KEY (CORRECT ANSWERS)

1. C	11. B
2. B	12. C
3. A	13. C
4. C	14. A
5. D	15. C
6. D	16. C
7. C	17. C
8. C	18. A
9. B	19. D
10. B	20. C

21. D
22. D
23. D
24. B
25. C

TEST 2

DIRECTIONS: Each question or incomplete statement is followed by several suggested answers or completions. Select the one that BEST answers the question or completes the statement. *PRINT THE LETTER OF THE CORRECT ANSWER IN THE SPACE AT THE RIGHT.*

1. Subject to federal trademark law, the use requirement for a service mark is generally satisfied by display 1.____

    A. on the premises where the services are actually rendered
    B. on products associated with, or used for the purpose of, rendering the registered services
    C. in the sale or advertising of the service (and the services so identified are actually rendered)
    D. on a printed receipt of payment for the services rendered

2. In an organizational buying center, the buying process is MOST often initiated by 2.____

    A. influencers   B. gatekeepers
    C. users   D. buyers

3. A company's sales of a product, stated as a percentage of an entire industry's sales of the product, is referred to as the company's 3.____

    A. channel spot   B. market share
    C. net percentage   D. sector

4. The concept of product life cycle generally influences marketing management in each of the following ways EXCEPT 4.____

    A. a firm must generate new products or enter new markets to sustain its profitability over time
    B. objectives and strategy for a given product change as it passes through various life-cycle stages
    C. opportunities and threats in each stage aid in the formulation of a most appropriate marketing mix for each stage of the life cycle
    D. products in the maturity stage serve as a model for companies to maintain near-constant brand loyalty

5. When a company decides to market a new product, the last step before commercialization is typically 5.____

    A. test marketing   B. business analysis
    C. product development D. in-home testing

6. What is the term for the combination of two or more stages of a marketing channel under one management? 6.____

    A. Consolidation
    B. Vertical channel integration
    C. Allocation
    D. Horizontal channel integration

7. What is the most centralized and formalized organizational form within a strategic business unit of a company?

   A. Product management
   B. Matrix
   C. Market management
   D. Functional

8. A marketing department divides an industrial market according to the organizational characteristics of the customers. This is an example of

   A. market aggregation strategy
   B. sectoring
   C. macrosegmentation
   D. microsegmentation

9. A large producer of paper goods decides to initiate a *count and recount* sales promotion among its resellers. The promotion LEAST likely to be successful would be for those resellers

   A. who have small warehouses
   B. operating within a limited geographic area
   C. who deal in perishable goods
   D. with large and unwieldy distribution channels

10. On a market research questionnaire, a subject is asked to state the degree to which he agrees with the statement:
    Cable television is too expensive.
    What type of assessment is being made?

    A. Protective technique
    B. Depth interview
    C. Attitude scale
    D. Balloon test

11. For a strategic business unit of a company that has adopted a low-cost defender strategy, the business unit will

    A. perform best on volume and share growth when the structure has low levels of formalization and centralization
    B. experience high levels of inter-functional conflict
    C. perform best on volume and share growth when the structure has a high level of specialization
    D. perform best on cash flow when controller, financial, and production managers have a substantial influence on business and marketing strategy decisions

12. In selecting a new trademark, a company's choice will be aided materially by

    A. using the trademark as a root to form other words for example, by adding the suffixes *-ize* or *-ate*
    B. making sure the trademark's correct grammatical classification is as a proper adjective
    C. simply using the name of the product as part of all of the trademark
    D. using the trademark as a proper noun whenever possible

13. A warehouse showroom is a retail facility characterized by each of the following EXCEPT

    A. large on-premise inventory
    B. vertical merchandise display space

C. use of warehouse materials-handling technology
D. separate customer service departments

14. In market research, the psychographic study is used primarily to

    A. compartmentalize the respondents into different market segments
    B. occupy the respondent while his or her real preferences and behaviors are determined
    C. ask the respondent to describe the behavior or preferences of his or her own social group
    D. ask the respondent to describe his or her own behavior, preferences, and lifestyle

15. The strategy of exclusive distribution is suitable for each of the following types of products EXCEPT those that

    A. are consumed over a long period of time
    B. exist in a limited market
    C. are frequently purchased
    D. require service or information to fit them to buyers' needs

16. _____ goods are characterized by high price, limited distribution, and strong advertising.

    A. Specialty   B. Durable
    C. Shopping   D. Unsought

17. An example of capital goods is

    A. office furniture   B. fork lift
    C. electric motor   D. stationery

18. A company decides to alter its marketing strategy by protecting its position in the market and minimizing its investment. The company is in a _____ competitive position and the market is _____ attractive.

    A. strong; moderately   B. moderately; not very
    C. weak; not very   D. weak; highly

19. The extra cost a firm incurs when it produces one more unit of a product is termed _____ cost.

    A. marginal   B. average fixed
    C. unit   D. average variable

20. Which of the following is a condition that would NOT be conducive toward a business's adoption of a *market analyzer* strategy?

    A. New-product applications still possible
    B. Substantial competition
    C. Technological advances still possible
    D. Industry in introductory or growth stage of the product life cycle

21. Which of the following is NOT a marketer-dominated source of information to which a consumer might consult before making a purchase?

    A. Salespersons   B. Free samples
    C. Packaging   D. Displays

22. Generally, the practice of offering quantity discounts to a consumer is beneficial in each of the following ways EXCEPT. 22._____

    A. lower inventory costs for the seller
    B. lower costs of transportation and handling
    C. provides the opportunity for flexible pricing
    D. encouraging customers to place more business with a single seller

23. A large manufacturer wishes to establish a multi-stage marketing channel for its product, but encounters difficulty in securing the services of intermediary agents or wholesalers. The most likely reason is that 23._____

    A. the manufacturer is in a geographically unfavorable location
    B. distribution among middlemen is dominated by another channel leader
    C. the manufacturer's service reputation is poor
    D. consumer demand for the product is low

24. If an intermediary in a marketing channel performs the function of assorting, the intermediary is 24._____

    A. combining products into collections that buyers want
    B. developing a bank or stock of homogeneous products to provide aggregate inventory
    C. classifying heterogeneous supplies into homogeneous groups
    D. breaking down homogeneous stocks into smaller units for wholesalers and retailers

25. Which of the following types of wholesalers would be LEAST likely to provide a producer with information about market conditions? 25._____

    A. Truck
    C. Drop shipper
    B. Rack jobber
    D. Cash and carry

KEY (CORRECT ANSWERS)

1. C
2. C
3. B
4. D
5. A

6. B
7. D
8. C
9. A
10. C

11. D
12. B
13. D
14. D
15. C

16. A
17. B
18. B
19. A
20. D

21. B
22. C
23. B
24. A
25. D

TEST 3

DIRECTIONS: Each question or incomplete statement is followed by several suggested answers or completions. Select the one that BEST answers the question or completes the statement. *PRINT THE LETTER OF THE CORRECT ANSWER IN THE SPACE AT THE RIGHT.*

1. The profits for a company offering a certain product become *excessive,* meaning the company has the power to restrict its output in the short term. The most likely result of this would be

    A. the gradual disappearance from other competitors from the market, who cannot afford to similarly restrict output
    B. the erosion of the company's economic power due to increased supply from competitors
    C. a lengthening and widening of the product line
    D. a near-monopoly on the market for the product

    1.____

2. An example of a direct cost is

    A. merchandising
    B. salesforce management
    C. general management
    D. cost of occupancy

    2.____

3. Person-specific factors influencing consumer buying decisions are

    A. psychological and motivational
    B. demographic and situational
    C. psychological and social
    D. demographic and motivational

    3.____

4. For a salesperson practicing technical selling, each of the following is generally considered to be an important personal characteristic EXCEPT

    A. education
    B. persuasiveness
    C. product knowledge
    D. customer knowledge

    4.____

5. During physical distribution of a product, which of the following functions is LEAST likely to be computerized?

    A. Order entry
    B. Freight bill payment
    C. Invoicing
    D. Site location

    5.____

6. For a marketing manager, the standard formula for improving cash flow management contains several elements. Which of the following is NOT one of these elements?

    A. Paying creditors quickly in order to eliminate interest costs
    B. Increasing the turnover of receivables by reducing the time taken by customers to pay their bills
    C. Reducing inventories
    D. Retaining a source of cash that requires no interest cost

    6.____

7. The satisfaction of a trademark's *use in commerce,* subject to federal trademark law, is generally provided by the

    A. shipment of goods bearing the trademark across state or national boundaries
    B. application for trademark registration

    7.____

C. affixation of the trademark to the products themselves, or to some portion of their containers or packaging
D. use of the registered trademark in advertising

8. Of all the methods used for analyzing marketing costs, the _____ cost approach is the least precise.

   A. full
   B. functional
   C. product-centered
   D. natural

9. Each of the following is an environmental factor that may influence an organization's buying behavior EXCEPT

   A. regulatory actions
   B. size and composition of buying center
   C. activities of interest groups
   D. inflation

10. For a business that adopts a prospecting strategy with respect to a certain market, which of the following policies would be most appropriate?

    A. Relatively narrow product lines
    B. Moderate to high trade promotion expenses as a percent of sales
    C. Relatively high degree of forward vertical integration
    D. Relatively low to competitive prices

11. Generally, the *mature* stage in a product's life cycle is characterized by

    A. large number of competitors
    B. high technical change in the product
    C. low profitability
    D. insignificant market growth rate

12. Dayton-Hudson, one of the country's largest retailers, has expanded from a regional department store into Target discount stores, B. Dalton bookstores, and several off-price fashion outlets.
    This is an example of

    A. horizontal channel integration
    B. accumulation
    C. vertical channel integration
    D. intensive distribution

13. A company might decide to engage in the practice of predatory pricing in order to

    A. segment a market in the early stages of a product life cycle
    B. generate a greater sales volume and lower production costs as much as possible
    C. enable a manufacturer to saturate a mass market quickly, before the competition can respond
    D. recover its high research-and-development costs more rapidly

14. A consumer displays the following patterns of buying behavior: He lives in a small house, favors national brands, spends more than other classes on household appliances, and is a heavy user of credit. According to market conventions, this consumer most likely occupies the _____ class.

    A. upper-middle
    B. lower-middle
    C. upper-lower
    D. lower-lower

15. Which of the following provisions was established by the Hart-Scott-Rodino Act of 1976?

    A. Prohibition of the acquisition of assets where the effect may be to create a monopoly
    B. Authorization of the FTC's issuance of trade regulation rules applicable to all members of an industry
    C. Authorization of FTC and Secretary of Health, Education and Welfare to issue regulations to ensure truthful disclosure of product identity and other relevant packaging practices
    D. Adoption of procedures to facilitate Department of Justice actions in antitrust actions

16. The MOST significant problem facing businesses who use the services of commission merchants is

    A. limited control over pricing
    B. short-term buyer-seller relationship
    C. limited geographic operations
    D. no delivery services

17. At different stages in a market's adoption of a new product, the role of personal influences is likely to be different. With this in mind, assume that the most influential source of information about a new farming product is U.S. Department of Agriculture field agent. The new product is most likely to be in the _____ stage of adoption.

    A. first awareness
    B. conception
    C. implementation
    D. decision

18. Typically, which of the following elements would appear LAST within an annual marketing plan?

    A. Key issues
    B. Projected profit-and-loss statement
    C. Controls
    D. Marketing strategy

19. According to the categories established by the VALS psychographic segments, the most disadvantaged Americans fall into the category of

    A. emulators
    B. sustainers
    C. belongers
    D. survivors

20. Over which of the following consumer buying selections would a reference group be LEAST likely to have influence?

    A. Cigarettes
    B. Insurance
    C. Canned peaches
    D. Headache remedy

21. One of the highest priorities for a producer in transporting its goods is security. If possible, which mode of transport should be selected?   21._____

    A. Air B. Water C. Rail D. Truck

22. The simplest and often most effective way for a company to increase profitability while maintaining its current product mix is to   22._____

    A. find new customers
    B. extend the product line
    C. increase consumption among present consumers
    D. find new uses for the product

23. It is generally true that as the number of units produced by a company increases,   23._____

    A. production cost per unit decreases
    B. the company's capital investment in the product decreases
    C. the market will become more competitive
    D. demand will moderately increase

24. Which of the following is categorized as a psychological influence on the consumer buying decision process?   24._____

    A. Culture and subcultures
    B. Perception
    C. Demographic factors
    D. Roles and family influences

25. A company compensates its sales staff with a combination of straight salary and commission. For the company, the most significant *disadvantage* to this approach is   25._____

    A. necessity of closer supervision of salespersons' activities
    B. potential administration difficulties
    C. selling expenses remain constant during sales declines
    D. sales manager may lose control over sales force

KEY (CORRECT ANSWERS)

1. B
2. A
3. B
4. B
5. D

6. A
7. A
8. D
9. B
10. B

11. D
12. A
13. B
14. C
15. D

16. A
17. C
18. C
19. D
20. C

21. B
22. C
23. A
24. B
25. B

TEST 4

DIRECTIONS: Each question or incomplete statement is followed by several suggested answers or completions. Select the one that BEST answers the question or completes the statement. *PRINT THE LETTER OF THE CORRECT ANSWER IN THE SPACE AT THE RIGHT.*

1. One of the differences between marketing and selling is that marketing

    A. is a one-way process
    B. uses informal planning and feedback
    C. emphasizes groups of consumers
    D. is volume-oriented

2. It is NOT true that organizational consumers

    A. purchase on the basis of specifications and technical data
    B. rarely lease equipment
    C. are more likely than final consumers to apply value and vendor analysis
    D. have shorter distribution channels than final consumers

3. Which of the following is NOT an advantage of national brands?

    A. Less complicated to administer than private brands
    B. They are presold
    C. They stimulate promotion through rebates
    D. Selling materials are provided with the product

4. If changes in price are exactly offset by changes in quantity demanded, keeping sales revenue constant, _____ demand exists.

    A. derived   B. elastic   C. scaled   D. unitary

5. A dealer brand

    A. is usually only available in the outlets of a single retailer
    B. generally has the lowest relative price
    C. is focused on generating manufacturer control
    D. is usually of less overall quality as the manufacturer's brand

6. Which of the following is a disadvantage associated with simple trend analysis as a means of sales forecasting?

    A. Markets not representative of all locations
    B. Does not provide a means of forecasting
    C. Economic decline not considered
    D. It assumes a constant market share

7. Which of the following is NOT a typical source of information for a company's total variable costs?

    A. Estimates of labor productivity
    B. Cost data from suppliers
    C. Bills
    D. Sales estimates

15

8. A company decides to enter a new market with an older product. What type of strategy should be used by the marketing department?

   A. Market development
   B. Product development
   C. Diversification
   D. Market penetration

9. Which of the following is NOT an advantage associated with chain ownership of retail outlets?

   A. Strong management
   B. Low investment costs
   C. Larger market
   D. Central purchasing

10. Each of the following is a reason why modification of an existing product package might be necessitated EXCEPT

    A. curtailment of the line
    B. changing target markets
    C. disjointed corporate identification
    D. need for countering competitive strategies

11. The pricing strategy that allows customers to purchase services on an optional basis is called _____ pricing.

    A. scatter
    B. unbundled
    C. skimming
    D. penetration

12. If a company makes a line of similar products or has one dominant line, the _____ organizational system is probably most appropriate.

    A. product-planning committee
    B. market ing-manager
    C. new-product manager
    D. product manager

13. What type of market research tool is a list of bipolar adjective scales, using the scales either in place of or in addition to open questions?

    A. Multidimensional scaling
    B. Nonprobability sampling
    C. Semantic differential
    D. Disguised survey

14. The management of American Furniture calculated that an overall investment of $550,000 was necessary in a given year to yield net sales of $930,000. The company's net profit was $110,000. Before taxes, the company's return on investment was

    A. 12%   B. 20%   C. 32%   D. 59%

15. The MAIN advantage associated with market share analysis is

    A. ability to pinpoint coming trends
    B. enabling an aggressive or declining company to adjust its forecast and marketing efforts
    C. enabling experts to direct, interpret, and respond to concrete data
    D. concentrated focus on consumer attitudes

16. A company's traffic manager   16._____

    A. controls the level and allocation of merchandise throughout the year
    B. consolidates small shipments from many companies
    C. is responsible for storage and movement of goods within a company's warehouse facilities
    D. is in charge of physical distribution

17. Which of the following is NOT a typical difference between the marketing characteristics   17._____
    of services and the marketing of goods?

    A. Consumer choice is more difficult with services because of intangibility
    B. Impossibility of separating the producer from the product
    C. Focus on consumer attitudes and behaviors is narrowed to single consumers
    D. Prevention of storage, and increased risk, associated with perishability

18. Which of the following is an order-generating cost?   18._____

    A. Advertising
    B. Merchandise handling
    C. Filling out and handling orders
    D. Computer time

19. Which of the following is NOT considered to be an internal barrier to future growth in service industries?   19._____

    A. Little emphasis on research and development
    B. Limited competition
    C. Overspecialization of personnel
    D. Small size of the average service firm

20. A company conducts its sales analysis by starting with general market information and   20._____
    then computing a series of more specific market information. This approach is known as

    A. test marketing   B. market buildup method
    C. simple trend analysis   D. chain-ratio method

21. NOT generally considered to be one of the primary components of a physical distribution   21._____
    system is a

    A. set of inventories of goods
    B. wholesaler who will oversee and direct the physical transport of the inventories
    C. set of fixed facilities at which goods are produced or stored
    D. transportation network connecting the fixed facilities, as well as with customer receiving points

22. What is the term for the number of different product lines offered by a company?   22._____

    A. Width   B. Depth
    C. Scope   D. Consistency

23. For a wide variety of products, a small proportion of total consumers may account for a large percentage of a product or service's total sales. This market segmentation concept is known as the

    A. concentric integration
    B. heavy-half
    C. iceberg principle
    D. ideal point

24. Which of the following promotional activities offers the highest flexibility?

    A. Advertising
    B. Personal selling
    C. Publicity
    D. Sales promotions

25. The use of market research alone for marketing information collection involves certain risks. Which of the following is NOT one of these risks?

    A. Actions are more likely to be reactionary than anticipatory
    B. Time lags when new research study is involved
    C. Ineffective review of marketing plans and decisions
    D. Incomplete idea of consumer attitudes

KEY (CORRECT ANSWERS)

1.	C	11.	B
2.	B	12.	B
3.	C	13.	C
4.	D	14.	B
5.	A	15.	B
6.	C	16.	D
7.	C	17.	C
8.	A	18.	A
9.	B	19.	C
10.	A	20.	D

21.	B
22.	A
23.	B
24.	B
25.	D

EXAMINATION SECTION
TEST 1

DIRECTIONS: Each question or incomplete statement is followed by several suggested answers or completions. Select the one that BEST answers the question or completes the statement. *PRINT THE LETTER OF THE CORRECT ANSWER IN THE SPACE AT THE RIGHT.*

1. During the maturity period of a product's life cycle, a company's strategic marketing objective will generally be to

    A. improve competitive position
    B. maintain position
    C. accelerate market growth
    D. harvest

2. A franchiser can MOST effectively minimize the risks of product liability by

    A. carefully preparing the trademark licensing agreement
    B. using an agent or broker to determine distribution
    C. constructing a multi-channel distribution system
    D. avoiding entanglement in claims against licensees

3. Which of the following is not an advantage associated with product management organizations?

    A. Improved coordination of functional activities within and across product-market entries
    B. Long-term orientation on the part of product managers
    C. Ability to identify and react more quickly to threats and opportunities faced by individual product-market entries

4. The retailing of service products differs from that of physical goods in each of the following ways EXCEPT

    A. more difficult consumer choice
    B. tendency toward localization
    C. easier quality control
    D. heterogeneous delivery process

5. A _____ is a name, term, or symbol which is intended to identify the goods or services of one seller or group of sellers and to differentiate them from those of competitors.

    A. patent   B. brand
    C. copyright   D. trademark

6. According to the categories established by the VALS psychographic segments, the smallest psychographic segment of Americans is the_____ category.

    A. achievers   B. experiential
    C. integrated   D. societally conscious

7. _____ is NOT typically a characteristic of department store retailers.

   A. Large sales volume
   B. Wide product mix
   C. Self-service outlets
   D. Achieve most sales through apparel and cosmetics

8. Face-to-face selling is likely to be of great importance under each of the following conditions EXCEPT

   A. a small target market consisting of relatively few customers
   B. a technically complex product or service
   C. the use of an extensive distribution network
   D. a marketing strategy aimed at wresting market share away from established competitors

9. A company wants to target a market that is highly competitive, but the company's competitive position is estimated to be only moderate by marketing advisers. Typically, which of the following should be part of the company's strategy?

   A. Invest to grow at maximum digestible rate
   B. Invest to improve position only in areas where risk is low
   C. Reinforce vulnerable areas
   D. Defend strengths

10. Which of the following is not a major INTERNAL variable that affects a company's ability to implement particular marketing strategies?

    A. Fit between individual product marketing strategies and the company's higher-level corporate and business strategies
    B. Administrative relationships between strategic business units and other members of the distribution channel
    C. Mechanisms used to coordinate and resolve conflicts among departments
    D. Contents of the detailed marketing action plan for each product-market entry

11. Each of the following is a projective technique for analyzing consumers' motives EXCEPT

    A. depth interviews
    B. sentence completion tests
    C. balloon tests
    D. word-association tests

12. As a selling objective, the gathering of information is especially useful in the

    A. maturity phase of consumer durables
    B. marketing of most shopping goods
    C. shakeout period of specialty markets
    D. introductory or growth stage of industrial products

13. A new lower-priced brand of shampoo is introduced into a highly competitive market by a competitor with limited resources. Companies with strong existing brands are likely to respond in each of the following ways EXCEPT

A. hold prices the same
B. offer coupons, discounts, or larger sizes at the same price
C. lower prices dramatically to drive the competitors out
D. lower prices to the level of the new brand

14. When marketing managers attempt to control marketing activities, they frequently encounter several problems. Which of the following is NOT typically one of these problems?   14.____

    A. Information required to control marketing activities is unavailable
    B. Internal cost analysis is unavailable
    C. Frequent and unpredictable changes in environmental factors
    D. Time lag between marketing activities and their effects

15. Each of the following is a typical characteristic of one-level marketing channels EXCEPT   15.____

    A. retail sales personnel must often exert pressure on shoppers
    B. extensive postsale servicing demand
    C. usually involve companies with limited distribution allocation
    D. retail sales personnel must be more knowledgeable about the product

16. Which of the following is NOT a limitation associated with the use of profitability analysis as a means of organizational control?   16.____

    A. Many objectives can best be measured in non-financial terms.
    B. Costs associated with specific marketing activities need to be analyzed in different market segments and distribution channels.
    C. Profits can be affected by factors over which management has no control.
    D. Profit is a short-term measure and can be manipulated by actions that may prove dysfunctional in the longer term.

17. A market aggregation strategy is appropriate where the total market   17.____

    A. uses limited distribution channels
    B. has few differences in customer needs or desires
    C. is organizational in nature
    D. is concentrated in one particular geographic location

18. A company produces a food seasoning that is widely used in restaurants. If the company decides to introduce this seasoning into supermarkets for home use, it is likely that the   18.____

    A. company has discovered a new market segment
    B. product has experienced a decline in restaurant sales
    C. product has been slightly modified
    D. product line has been widened

19. Which of the following is NOT usually a type of organizational purchase?   19.____

    A. Discretionary purchase   B. Straight rebuy
    C. Modified rebuy   D. New-task purchase

20. In a growth market situation, a company defines its primary marketing objective as attracting a smaller share of new customers in a variety of smaller, specialized segments where customers' needs or preferences differ from those of early adopters in the mass market.
    The company's marketing strategy could best be described as

    A. encirclement
    B. guerrilla attack
    C. leapfrog
    D. frontal attack

21. Contractual systems sponsored by wholesalers, which independent retailers can join, are known as

    A. manufacturer-sponsored franchises
    B. cooperative chains
    C. administered systems
    D. voluntary chains

22. The practice of skimming pricing is MOST likely to be used in the marketing of

    A. high-technology products
    B. clothing
    C. franchised restaurants
    D. low-margin household products

23. The institution with the authority to deal with trademark infringements is the

    A. Federal Trade Commission
    B. municipal, county, or state court
    C. Department of Commerce
    D. Patent and Trademark Office

24. In the relationship between a business unit and the company within which it operates, *centralization* refers to the

    A. location of decision authority and control within an organization's hierarchy
    B. degree to which decisions and working relationships are governed by formal rules and standard policies
    C. geographic location of the business unit in relation to the administrative center of the company
    D. division of tasks and activities across positions within the organizational unit

25. A leading stationery manufacturer, due to the large demand for its product, was able to force less desirable lines upon retailers, who had to accept these lines in order to receive the fast-moving items. Eventually, the manufacturer experienced an off-year, and the retailers struck back by refusing to take any items they did not want, even buying only minimal amounts of the faster-moving items. This situation is an example of

    A. trust-busting
    B. an administered system
    C. the natural retail cycle
    D. channel conflict

KEY (CORRECT ANSWERS)

1. B
2. A
3. C
4. C
5. B

6. C
7. C
8. A
9. C
10. B

11. A
12. D
13. C
14. B
15. C

16. B
17. B
18. A
19. A
20. A

21. D
22. A
23. B
24. A
25. D

TEST 2

DIRECTIONS: Each question or incomplete statement is followed by several suggested answers or completions. Select the one that BEST answers the question or completes the statement. *PRINT THE LETTER OF THE CORRECT ANSWER IN THE SPACE AT THE RIGHT.*

1. A company might decide to engage in the practice of penetration pricing in order to   1.____

    A. increase market share and gain greater visibility and market power
    B. create a high-quality image for the product
    C. clear out inventories of older models
    D. discourage potential competitors from entering the market at all

2. When a buyer questions whether he or she should have purchased a product at all, or would have been better off purchasing another brand, this is an example of   2.____

    A. demarketing   B. cognitive dissonance
    C. consumerism   D. evoked set

3. The primary responsibility of a company's sales force is to gain and maintain support for the company's products within the distribution channel by providing merchandising and promotional services to the channel members. The company's sales force is MOST likely composed of _____ sellers.   3.____

    A. new business   B. missionary
    C. technical   D. trade

4. Under the Uniform Commercial Code, certain remedies are available to a party in a sales contract who claim a breach of the contract. The code sets forth each of the following specific measures for ascertaining the amount of damages to goods named in such a contract EXCEPT the _____ standard.   4.____

    A. resale   B. actual cash value
    C. market value   D. profit

5. A company has adopted a prospector strategy for entrance into a certain market. Typically, a business unit in the company will perform best when one of its functional strengths is   5.____

    A. production   B. distribution
    C. financial management and control   D. marketing

6. _____ is the specific term for the entity that permits the identification of goods as the product of a particular maker, seller, or sponsor.   6.____

    A. patent   B. trademark
    C. copyright   D. brand

7. A group of smaller hotel chains finds that they can make a reasonable profit by following the prices of the price leader – a large, nationwide chain as long as they can keep their hotels reasonably well-filled. To do this, the smaller chains advertise heavily and try to book as many meetings, conventions, and tours as possible.
This is an example of   7.____

    A. imitation   B. market saturation
    C. nonprice competition   D. leader pricing

24

8. Which of the following consumer selections is likely to be nost strongly influenced by a reference group?

   A. Radio
   B. Coffee
   C. Automobile
   D. Magazine or book

9. Generally, the practice of offering seasonal discounts to a consumer is beneficial in each of the following ways EXCEPT

   A. lower inventory carrying costs for the seller
   B. less overload on distribution facilities
   C. encourages buyer to pay as soon as possible
   D. less overtime pay for employees

10. The first introduction of a graphite golf club into the market was an example of

    A. adaptive replacement
    B. product innovation
    C. imitation
    D. line simplification

11. According to market research conventions, which of the following qualities or behaviors would be displayed by members of the lower-middle class?

    A. Tend to be brand loyal
    B. Buy relatively expensive homes to indicate social position
    C. Avoid mass merchandisers
    D. Common joint shopping of husband and wife

12. In a marketing audit, a company focuses on whether the company has adequate and timely information about consumers' satisfaction with its products. Which area of the company's marketing activities is being audited?

    A. Planning and control system
    B. Organization
    C. Objectives and strategy
    D. Marketing environment

13. A credit-card company decides to segment its market using a product-related approach. Most likely, the users will be segmented according to

    A. their level of disposable income
    B. the types of goods and services they use their cards for
    C. the frequency with which they use their cards
    D. the pattern of credit services they utilize

14. A personal characteristic considered to be important for missionary sellers is

    A. knowledge of customers
    B. maturity
    C. verbal skill
    D. empathy

15. Under the Uniform Commercial Code, the parties in a sales contract can conclude a contract for sale even if the price has not been settled. In such a case, the price will be considered to be a reasonable price at the time of delivery under any of the following conditions EXCEPT

    A. the price is to be fixed in good faith by the buyer or seller
    B. nothing at all has been said as to price
    C. the price is definitively scheduled for consideration by an impartial arbitrator
    D. the price is yet to be agreed upon by the parties and they fail to agree

16. A strategic business unit within a company desires a high level of autonomy within the organization. Which type of business strategy would be most conducive to this?

   A. Prospector
   B. Analyzer
   C. Differentiated defender
   D. Low-cost defender

17. In a certain marketing channel network, a wholesaler's markup on a certain product is 20%, and the retailer's markup is 50%. An end-use customer pays $300 for the product. What was the price at which the wholesaler purchased the product from the producer?

   A. $150   B. $166.67   C. $200   D. $233.34

18. Under the Uniform Commercial Code, certain remedies are available to a party in a sales contract who claim a breach of the contract. Generally, which of the following remedies is NOT available to the buyer in such a contract?

   A. Purchase of substitute goods, holding seller liable for any reasonable losses the buyer might have incurred in the cover operation
   B. Cancel the contract entirely, and recover moneys which might have been paid, as well as recovering damages
   C. Sue for possession of the goods
   D. Acceptance of nonconforming goods and suing for compensatory damages as well as punitive damages

19. A _____ is most likely to extend credit to customers.

   A. selling agent
   B. manufacturer's agent
   C. commission merchant
   D. broker

20. In exercising control over inventory, it is important to remember that individual reorders depend on

   A. the probability of obsolescence
   B. the trade-off between the cost of carrying larger inventories and the cost of processing small orders
   C. the total amount of capital tied up in inventory
   D. overall demand

21. The PRIMARY difference between a facilitating agency and a marketing channel member is that a facilitating agency

   A. does not perform negotiating functions
   B. is less specialized
   C. is not involved with physical distribution of a product
   D. has no influence over pricing

22. Most business firms judge their effectiveness in terms of

   A. total revenue
   B. profits as a percentage of sales
   C. segments controlled
   D. return on investment (ROI)

23. A market segmentation study describes a certain population as *typical light users* of the product under investigation. In this example, the study is using a _____ descriptor. 23._____

   A. customer needs
   B. person-related behavioral
   C. product-related behavioral
   D. demographic

24. Under which of the following conditions is a personal selling strategy targeted toward the development of new customers most appropriate? 24._____

   A. The product is in the introductory stage
   B. Business is pursuing a differentiated defender strategy
   C. Firm intentions to increase market share of a mature market
   D. Lengthy purchase decision process

25. Generally, the more conspicuous a product is, the more likely it is that a consumer's brand decision will be influenced by 25._____

   A. reference groups   B. family roles
   C. situational factors   D. demographics

KEY (CORRECT ANSWERS)

1. D
2. B
3. D
4. B
5. D

6. B
7. C
8. C
9. C
10. A

11. D
12. A
13. B
14. C
15. C

16. A
17. B
18. D
19. A
20. B

21. A
22. D
23. C
24. C
25. A

TEST 3

DIRECTIONS: Each question or incomplete statement is followed by several suggested answers or completions. Select the one that BEST answers the question or completes the statement. *PRINT THE LETTER OF THE CORRECT ANSWER IN THE SPACE AT THE RIGHT.*

1. Each of the following is a reason why marketing channels in a distribution system might change EXCEPT

    A. one or more middlemen find a way to increase their own profits or strength in the channel
    B. new technology
    C. one or more companies discover a less expensive way to distribute their goods
    D. greater customer service provisions offered by a company

    1.____

2. A blended *Scotch* whiskey, made in the United States, is priced at a low margin, and sells poorly. After the manufacturer raises the price of the product by $2 a bottle, without any change in the product or its packaging, sales increase dramatically.
   This can be best explained by asserting that customers

    A. believe the product offers greater prestige
    B. mistakenly believe the product is a single-malt Scotch
    C. believe the quality of the product to be comparable to that of higher-priced whiskeys
    D. are more likely to believe the product was imported from Scotland

    2.____

3. A well-established personal computer manufacturer with several product lines introduces a new line of computers at a very low price, and receives an estimated $10 billion in orders before the machines are available at retail outlets. The introduction of this product line will most likely result in a *decrease* in the company's sales by

    A. discouraging competition that will supply long-term technological growth to the market
    B. starting a price war with competitors
    C. encouraging the proliferation of a horizontal marketing channel structure
    D. drawing customer attention away from other, higher-margin product lines

    3.____

4. In establishing physical distribution objectives, the distribution-center concept has a few distinct advantages. Which of the following is NOT one of these advantages?

    A. Greater control over shipments
    B. Justified expenditures on automated equipment for more efficient handling
    C. Lower total cost
    D. Goods can be shipped directly from producer in the form or number ordered by customers

    4.____

5. A company may want to use a salesforce compensation plan combining both salary and commission when

    A. company cannot closely control salesforce activities
    B. sales territories have relatively similar sales potentials
    C. when salespersons need to perform many non-selling activities
    D. highly aggressive selling is required

    5.____

29

6. Which of the following goods are characterized by limited availability, an emphasis on personal selling, and availability in a limited number of stores?

    A. Specialty
    B. Convenience
    C. Shopping
    D. Unsought

7. A company's pricing practice interacts with promotion expenditures in many ways. Which of the following statements is NOT true in the case of advertising for consumer products?

    A. Higher prices for a new type of consumer product can provide the funds necessary to advertise heavily, in order to inform people of the improved benefits offered by the new product.
    B. Advertising often has a greater effect on the sales of high-priced than low-priced products.
    C. Higher advertising expenditures can reduce the total cost of selling by preselling the buyer.
    D. Companies that want to support a high price for their product often spend a great deal on advertising.

8. When making purchase decisions, resellers typically consider each of the following factors EXCEPT

    A. amount of space required to handle a product
    B. lowest acceptable bid for products or services
    C. supplier's ability to provide adequate quantities when needed
    D. product demand

9. Generally, due to potential changes in cash flow and production practices, which department in a company would have the EASIEST time accepting a decision to simplify a product line?

    A. Higher-level management
    B. Sales
    C. Production
    D. Finance

10. In pinpointing the essential tasks of distribution, the producer must keep in mind the basic trade-relations mix. Which of the following is NOT an element of the trade-relations mix?

    A. Conditions of sale
    B. Price policy
    C. Trademark status
    D. Territorial rights

11. During the shakeout period of a product's life cycle, a company's investments in the product (R&D, working capital, and marketing) will generally be

    A. negative   B. low   C. moderate   D. high

12. A registered trademark can be made incontestable as soon as it has been in use, subsequent to the date of the certificate, for

    A. 6 months   B. 1 year   C. 5 years   D. 10 years

13. A large snack-food company periodically experiences declines in the sales of its products. In the long term, the company can probably BEST counteract the decrease in profits by

    A. spending more on promotion and advertising
    B. shifting its promotion and advertising to other market segments
    C. periodically introducing new product lines
    D. periodically changing the packaging of its products

14. According to the categories established by the VALS psychographic segments, most Americans fall into the category

    A. achievers
    B. belongers
    C. societally conscious
    D. emulators

15. In a single year, company X sold $800,000 worth of its product. The entire industry sold a total of $9 million. What was the approximate market share of company X for this product in this year?

    A. .09%   B. 8.9%   C. 11.1%   D. 17.8%

16. Each of the following is a reason why a retailer might practice scrambled merchandising EXCEPT

    A. generation of more traffic
    B. generating brand loyalty
    C. increasing impulse purchases
    D. realizing higher profit margins

17. When a business faces an extremely complex and uncertain environment, which form of organization is MOST likely to be appropriate?

    A. Matrix
    B. Product management
    C. Market management
    D. Functional

18. The exemption of dedicated export-trade associations from existing antitrust legislation is the major provision of the_____ Act.

    A. Webb-Pomerene
    B. Clayton
    C. Robinson-Patman
    D. Federal Trade Commission

19. For a business that has adopted a differentiated defender strategy with respect to a certain market, which of the following policies would be LEAST appropriate?

    A. High salesforce expenditure as a percent of sales
    B. Relatively high prices
    C. Broad, technically sophisticated product lines
    D. Low trade promotion expenses as a percent of sales

20. Which of the following is categorized as a social influence on the consumer buying decision process?

    A. Personality
    B. Reference group
    C. Attitude
    D. Job status (promotion, firing, etc.)

21. A company's marketing department adopts the communication of product information as one of its primary selling objectives.
    Which of the following is LEAST likely to be true? The

    A. product is technically complex
    B. purchase decision is typically a lengthy process
    C. product is in the maturity stage of its life cycle
    D. purchase decision is influenced by multiple factors

22. In terms of trademark law, most foreign countries differ from the United States *primarily* in the

    A. means by which infringement is litigated
    B. legal definition of a trademark
    C. requirement of use as a prerequisite to registration
    D. distinction between a trademark and a service mark

23. Which of the following is an example of an indirect cost?

    A. Materials
    B. General management
    C. Advertising
    D. Labor

24. The tendency to remain loyal to a company rather than a particular brand or product is known as

    A. evoked set
    B. discrimination
    C. mental set
    D. generalization

25. The purpose of *push money* is to

    A. provide an incentive to retail sales personnel
    B. encourage transport agents to pay freight costs
    C. encourage customer trade-ins
    D. provide a buying incentive to customers

KEY (CORRECT ANSWERS)

1. D
2. C
3. D
4. D
5. B

6. C
7. B
8. B
9. A
10. C

11. C
12. C
13. C
14. B
15. B

16. B
17. A
18. A
19. C
20. B

21. C
22. C
23. B
24. D
25. A

TEST 4

DIRECTIONS: Each question or incomplete statement is followed by several suggested answers or completions. Select the one that BEST answers the question or completes the statement. *PRINT THE LETTER OF THE CORRECT ANSWER IN THE SPACE AT THE RIGHT.*

1. The total costs of producing an additional quantity of a product, less the total costs of producing the current quantity, will yield the _____ costs. 1._____

    A. total
    B. average total
    C. marginal
    D. total variable

2. Each of the following is a consideration associated with the profitability factor of a business analysis EXCEPT 2._____

    A. time to recoup initial costs
    B. risk
    C. control over price
    D. potential sales at different prices

3. A strategy in which one name is used for several products is known as _____ branding. 3._____

    A. family   B. net   C. line   D. wide

4. Which of the following is NOT a common means of preventing or resolving channel conflict? 4._____

    A. Proper channel design
    B. Selective distribution
    C. Employment of cooperation techniques
    D. Exertion of power

5. Which of the following is a disadvantage associated with the sales force survey as a means of sales forecasting? 5._____

    A. Assumption that areas will behave similarly in the future
    B. Does not reveal traits of heavy users
    C. Lack of awareness of competitor's intentions
    D. Regions nor representative

6. Which of the following is typically controlled by a company's top management, rather than by the marketing department? 6._____

    A. Role of marketing decisions
    B. Selection of target markets
    C. Profit objectives
    D. Type of marketing organization

7. A disadvantage associated with independent ownership of a retail outlet is 7._____

    A. inflexibility
    B. much competition
    C. limited decision-making ability
    D. high investment costs

8. Advertising will dominate in a company's promotional mix when

   A. products are simple and inexpensive, and differential advantages are clear
   B. the market is small and concentrated, and organized consumers are involved
   C. customers expect assistance and service in retail stores
   D. the budget is limited or tailored to the needs of specific customers

9. Which of the following factors is NOT used to calculate the, target price of a product?

   A. Standard volume
   B. Variable per unit costs
   C. Investment costs
   D. Target ROI percentage

10. A manufacturer's brand

    A. is not widely advertised
    B. is targeted to price-conscious consumers
    C. has a price usually controlled by the dealer
    D. is usually part of a deep product line

11. Which of the following steps in a segmentation strategy would typically be performed FIRST?

    A. Establishing an appropriate marketing plan
    B. Selecting consumer segments
    C. Analyzing consumer similarities and differences
    D. Developing consumer group profiles

12. A company's retail merchandise manager

    A. supervises several buyers
    B. supervises the day-to-day activities of the store
    C. is responsible for purchasing items for resale
    D. is a buyer for a manufacturer, wholesaler, or retailer

13. Which of the following market research techniques would typically be best for discovering consumer attitudes?

    A. Simulation
    B. Survey
    C. Experimentation
    D. Observation

14. The MOST significant in number and volume of those engaged in the wholesaling business are

    A. merchant wholesalers
    B. assemblers
    C. manufacturer's sales branches
    D. merchandise agents and brokers

15. Which of the following types of organizational consumer decision processes involves the greatest amount of perceived risk?

    A. Impulse buy
    B. New task purchase
    C. Modified rebuy
    D. Straight rebuy

16. Each of the following is a consideration associated with the demand projection factor of a business analysis EXCEPT

    A. speed of consumer acceptance
    B. channel intensity
    C. per unit fixed costs
    D. seasonally of sales

17. Which of the following questions would appear on a disguised market research survey?

    A. At what time of day do you usually eat dinner?
    B. Which of the following is most important to you?
    C. What factors do you consider in the purchase of home furnishings?
    D. Are people who purchase sports cars status conscious;

18. Most franchisors require each of the following of a franchisee EXCEPT

    A. college education
    B. age 26-60
    C. owning one's own home
    D. able to finance leasehold improvements

19. A company conducts its sales analysis by gathering small, separate market segments and then aggregating them. This approach is known as

    A. consumer survey
    B. market buildup method
    C. simple trend analysis
    D. chain-ratio method

20. $\frac{\text{Cost of goods sold}}{\text{Net sales}}$ is a formula for which performance ratio?

    A. Stock turnover ratio
    B. Cost of goods sold ratio
    C. Return on investment
    D. Sales efficiency ratio

21. What is the term for the number of product items within each of the product lines offered by a company?

    A. Width   B. Depth   C. Scope   D. Consistency

22. In organizational purchasing for middlemen, the search for sources can have a large number of influences. Which of the following is NOT typically one of these influences?

    A. Past dates of sales for similar products
    B. Consumer surveys
    C. Shopping competitors' offerings
    D. Market research studies

23. What is the term for a form of price adjustment in which across-the-board price increases are published to supplement list prices?

    A. Bundling   B. Surcharge   C. Stimulus   D. Tariff

24. Which of the following promotional activities has the LOWEST overall cost per potential customer?

    A. Sales promotion
    B. Publicity
    C. Advertising
    D. Personal selling

25. In the multiple segmentation method for developing a target market,   25.____
    A. there is one product or service brand tailored to one consumer group
    B. there is a distinct price range for each consumer group
    C. a mass media promotion is used
    D. the object is a broad range of consumers

KEY (CORRECT ANSWERS)

1. C
2. D
3. A
4. B
5. C

6. A
7. B
8. A
9. B
10. D

11. C
12. A
13. B
14. A
15. B

16. C
17. D
18. A
19. B
20. B

21. B
22. B
23. B
24. C
25. B

EXAMINATION SECTION
TEST 1

DIRECTIONS: Each question or incomplete statement is followed by several suggested answers or completions. Select the one that BEST answers the question or completes the statement. *PRINT THE LETTER OF THE CORRECT ANSWER IN THE SPACE AT THE RIGHT.*

1. The term of a federal trademark registration is

   A. 10 years
   B. 20 years
   C. until the company stops using the trademark for any purpose
   D. indefinite

2. Generally, the most significant basis for product liability is the potential liability for

   A. design defects
   B. manner of complaint handling
   C. misrepresentation
   D. distribution decisions

3. _____ goods are not an example of convenience products.

   A. Impulse
   B. Unsought
   C. Staple
   D. All of the above

4. The marketing channel *produoer→ retailer→ consumer* is MOST comnonly used in the distribution of

   A. agricultural produce
   B. automobiles
   C. refrigerators
   D. candy

5. Market segmentation CANNOT

   A. identify opportunities for new-product development
   B. reflect the realities faced by companies in most markets
   C. help in the design of products and marketing programs that are most effective for reaching heterogeneous groups of customers
   D. improve the strategic allocation of marketing resources

6. According to market research conventions, which of the following qualities or behaviors would be displayed by members of the lower-lower class?

   A. Spend a relatively larger proportion of income on household items
   B. Prefers to shop at nonexclusive department stores
   C. Spend a relatively larger proportion of income on products to improve personal appearance
   D. Respectability a major objective

7. Which of the following strategic marketing objectives is used during the shakeout period of a product's life cycle?

   A. Hold share
   B. Harvest
   C. Stimulate primary demand
   D. Build share

8. Mass merchandisers, as compared to department stores,

    A. are more service-oriented
    B. have a shallower product mix
    C. appeal to homogeneous target markets
    D. have a narrower product mix

9. Each of the following is an example of process goods EXCEPT

    A. thermostats for refrigerators
    B. truck tires
    C. portable drills
    D. sheet steel

10. A *dealer loader* is

    A. an advertisement that promotes a product and identifies the names of participating retailers who sell the product
    B. a gift given to a retailer who purchases a specified quantity of merchandise
    C. used to promote a line of goods by providing additional compensation to salespeople
    D. a manufacturer's agreement to pay resellers certain amounts of money for providing special promotional efforts such as advertising or displays

11. Which of the following is NOT a kind of full-service wholesaler?

    A. General merchandise
    B. Mail order
    C. Specialty-line
    D. Limited-line

12. From a marketing planning standpoint, there are three major strategic options most companies have under conditions of a kinked demand curve. Which of the following is NOT one of these options?

    A. Change both price and one or more other elements of the marketing mix
    B. Stay at the market price, but change one or more element of the marketing mix
    C. Lower production costs for a particular product and stay at the market price
    D. Raise or lower prices to maximize short-term profits on the basis of the kinked curve

13. A manufacturer experiences high transportation costs, but low storage costs in the physical distribution of its product. Which of the following transport modes is probably being used by the company?

    A. Rail
    B. Truck
    C. Air
    D. Water

14. Which of the following is an example of a producer market?

    A. A hospital buying tongue depressors
    B. A wholesaler buying lumber for resale to a hardware franchise
    C. The Postal Service buying wood pulp for stamp production
    D. A grocery store buying paper bags for customer purchases

15. A _____ set is the term used to denote a group of brands that a buyer views as possible alternatives after a successful information search.

    A. mental   B. inert   C. inept   D. evoked

16. Five buyers consistently purchase the products of five producers. If an intermediary serves both producers and buyers, the number of transactions necessary to provide buyers with their products can be reduced to

    A. 2   B. 5   C. 10   D. 25

17. A marketing department groups customers according to the characteristics of the individuals who influence purchasing decisions. This is an example of

    A. psychographics
    B. focus grouping
    C. macrosegmentation
    D. microsegmentation

18. In an automobile showroom, a salesperson informs a customer of a car's highly successful EPA mileage rating. The customer does not believe the salesperson, and soon forgets all about the car's rating.
    This is an example of

    A. selective retention
    B. self-fulfilling prophecy
    C. selective distortion
    D. cognitive dissonance

19. In an organizational buying center, the final authority over buying decisions is held by

    A. deciders
    B. gatekeepers
    C. users
    D. buyers

20. Which of the following personal characteristics is MOST likely to be useful to a trade seller?

    A. Product knowledge
    B. Aggressiveness
    C. Technical ability
    D. Knowledge of customers

21. A marketing department determines that a certain product is in the declining phase. The company should probably

    A. narrow the product line
    B. rationalize the line or eliminate weaker items
    C. reduce the length of the line
    D. hold the length of the line

22. Each of the following are examples of specialty goods EXCEPT

    A. office furniture
    B. automobiles
    C. designer clothing
    D. personal computers

23. If an industrial buyer is offered a cash discount of *2/10 net 30* after purchasing a product, the

    A. buyer will receive a 20% discount if the bill is paid within 30 days
    B. buyer agrees to pay in 2 cash installments of $10 within 30 days
    C. bill must be paid in full within 30 days
    D. buyer must pay in cash

24. A consumer sees an advertisement by a toothpaste producer claiming that one-third of the people using their product have fewer cavities. The consumer takes this claim to mean that two-thirds of the people who use the product have more cavities.
This is an example of

    A. selective retention
    B. cognitive dissonance
    C. selective distortion
    D. mental set

24.____

25. Each of the following is a way in which a private warehouse facility differs from a public warehouse EXCEPT

    A. private warehouses are usually leased
    B. private warehouses involve fixed costs
    C. public warehouses do not establish field warehouses
    D. public warehouses provide bonded storage

25.____

KEY (CORRECT ANSWERS)

1.	B		11.	B
2.	A		12.	C
3.	B		13.	C
4.	B		14.	D
5.	C		15.	D
6.	C		16.	C
7.	D		17.	D
8.	B		18.	A
9.	C		19.	A
10.	B		20.	D

21. C
22. A
23. C
24. C
25. C

TEST 2

DIRECTIONS: Each question or incomplete statement is followed by several suggested answers or completions. Select the one that BEST answers the question or completes the statement. *PRINT THE LETTER OF THE CORRECT ANSWER IN THE SPACE AT THE RIGHT.*

1. Generally, the MOST significant problem associated with unreliable transport services is   1._____

   A. high inventory
   B. lack of security
   C. longer delivery lead times
   D. lower margin

2. Each of the following is a sales promotion aimed primarily at resellers EXCEPT   2._____

   A. dealer loaders
   B. push money
   C. point-of-purchase displays
   D. buying allowances

3. Which of the following is NOT a characteristic of the growth stage of a product's life cycle?   3._____

   A. Large profitability
   B. Moderate technical change in product
   C. Few to many market segments
   D. Limited competition

4. Which of the following types of wholesalers will NOT take physical possession of a producer's merchandise?   4._____

   A. Mail order   B. Rack jobber
   C. Drop shipper   D. Cash and carry

5. A company wants to target a market that is moderately competitive, and the company's competitive position is estimated to be very strong by marketing advisers. Typically, which of the following should be part of the company's strategy?   5._____

   A. Build up ability to counter competition
   B. Specialize around limited strengths
   C. Minimize investments and focus operations
   D. Invest to grow at maximum digestible rate

6. A company producing relatively low-priced watches decides to seek widespread distribution through drugstores and discount stores, because many jewelers will not accept the lower relative markup of the company's watches, and because most other watches are being sold through jewelry stores.   6._____
   In this case, the company's distribution strategy was decided primarily by

   A. the nature of the product
   B. company resources
   C. competitors' distribution strategies
   D. the nature of the market

7. A marketing department decides to conduct marketing research using the exploratory design. Which of the following will probably NOT be used as a source for this research?

    A. Interviews with knowledgeable people
    B. Secondary data
    C. Experimental research studies
    D. Case studies

8. Which of the following is generally considered to be the personal characteristic that would be LEAST important for a salesperson practicing new business selling?

    A. Empathy   B. Experience
    C. Age   D. Aggressiveness

9. Motives that influence where a person purchases products on a regular basis are commonly called _____ motives.

    A. projected   B. patronage
    C. learning   D. circadian

10. A company decides to conduct an audit of its marketing environment. Which of the following questions is it likely to ask?

    A. Which opportunities or threats emerge from within the company?
    B. Does the organizational structure fit the evolving needs of the marketplace?
    C. How effective are each of the major marketing activities?
    D. How well do the products/brands meet the needs of the target markets?

11. Which of the following is the federal legislation governing the establishment and use of trademarks?

    A. Lanham Act
    B. Celler-Kefauver Act
    C. Clayton Act
    D. Fair Packaging and Labeling Law

12. Which of the following is a person-specific influence on the consumer buying decision process?

    A. Perception   B. Learning
    C. Social class   D. Marital status

13. Market segmentation has become increasingly important in developing business and marketing strategies for each of the following reasons EXCEPT

    A. a decreasing trend in population growth
    B. increasingly diverse customer needs
    C. decreasing trend in disposable incomes
    D. increasing consumer awareness through media advancements

14. A company might decide to engage in the practice of skimming pricing in order to

    A. clear out excess inventories of older models
    B. keep demand low enough to be filled by a company's productive capacity
    C. drive some of the smaller competitors out of the market
    D. enter a market already dominated by other companies

15. Each of the following is a typical provision of a trademark licensing agreement EXCEPT

    A. assurance not to sue the user if conditions of the agreement are met
    B. geographical or other limitations or requirements of the use of the mark
    C. requirement of royalty payments to licensor for use of the mark
    D. licensee control over the nature and quality of licensed product or services

16. Agents are appropriate in industrial channels for each of the following conditions EXCEPT when

    A. selling functions are important
    B. the buyer is extremely large
    C. products are standardized
    D. information gathering is important

17. Within a company that has adopted a low-cost defender business strategy,

    A. there is relatively little synergy
    B. performance is likely to be best when marketing, R&D, and manufacturing facilities are shared with other business units in the company
    C. individual business units operate with a relatively high degree of autonomy
    D. a business unit manager's compensation is typically based on share growth

18. A _____ is most likely to take physical possession of a producer's merchandise.

    A. commission merchant   B. selling agent
    C. manufacturer's agent   D. broker

19. Under the terms of federal regulations, it is NOT a justifiable reason for offering different prices to different wholesalers for the same product when

    A. it can be proven that the cost of selling to one customer were the same or less than the difference in price
    B. goods are deteriorating or obsolete
    C. a lower price was offered to markedly undercut a competitive offer from another seller
    D. the goods are of different grade and quality

20. Which of the following is NOT a typical way in which organizational transactions differ from consumer sales?

    A. More reciprocity
    B. Less frequent negotiation
    C. Involve more buyers
    D. Longer negotiation periods needed to complete sales

21. The main difference between the full-cost and direct-cost methods for determining marketing costs is that the

    A. direct-cost method does not use non-traceable common costs
    B. direct-cost method uses costs attributable to the performance of marketing functions
    C. full-cost method does not use direct costs
    D. full-cost method uses marketing function accounts

22. One of the highest priorities for a producer in transporting its goods is traceability. If possible, which mode of transport should be selected? 22.____

    A. Air   B. Water   C. Rail   D. Truck

23. The abandonment of a given product line is a strategy that should be considered by a company 23.____

    A. during the introductory stage in the product life cycle
    B. during the maturity stage
    C. during the shakeout stage
    D. at every stage in the product life cycle

24. A company has adopted a prospector strategy for entrance into a certain market. For a business unit within the company, it would NOT be true that the unit will 24.____

    A. perform best when formalization is high
    B. perform best when controller, financial, and production managers have a substantial influence on business and marketing strategy decisions
    C. experience high levels of interfunctional conflict
    D. perform best when its functional strengths include sales, product R&D, and engineering

25. A company experiences a rapidly decreasing growth rate in sales of a certain product that results in strong price competition, after which many firms are forced to exit the market. In terms of the product life cycle concept, this situation illustrates the _____ stage or period. 25.____

    A. growth   B. decline   C. mature   D. shakeout

KEY (CORRECT ANSWERS)

1. A
2. C
3. D
4. C
5. A

6. C
7. C
8. A
9. B
10. A

11. A
12. D
13. C
14. B
15. D

16. B
17. B
18. A
19. C
20. C

21. A
22. A
23. D
24. A
25. D

TEST 3

DIRECTIONS: Each question or incomplete statement is followed by several suggested answers or completions. Select the one that BEST answers the question or completes the statement. *PRINT THE LETTER OF THE CORRECT ANSWER IN THE SPACE AT THE RIGHT.*

1. The primary responsibility of a company's sales force is to build and maintain volume from current customers by giving purchase decision makers product information and service assistance.
   The sales force is MOST likely composed of _____ sellers.   1.____

   A. new business   B. missionary
   C. technical   D. trade

2. Which of the following sectors is most likely to achieve sales through a franchising arrangement?   2.____

   A. Gasoline service stations
   B. Fast-food restaurants
   C. Soft-drink bottlers
   D. Automotive products and services

3. Each of the following is an advantage of compensating sales employees with straight commissions EXCEPT: 3.____

   A. Selling expenses are directly related to sales resources
   B. It permits sales managers to push certain items
   C. It gives sales manager large amount of control over sales staff
   D. There is maximum incentive for sales

4. The strategy of selective distribution would MOST likely be successful with   4.____

   A. specialty goods   B. convenience goods
   C. low-margin services   D. durable goods

5. Each of the following is a clear sign that inventory is not in control EXCEPT   5.____

   A. consistently long delivery lead times
   B. large inventory write-offs
   C. inventory growing at a slower rate than sales
   D. surplus inventory

6. Which of the following is categorized as a situational influence on the consumer buying decision process?   6.____

   A. Marital status   B. Health status
   C. Social class   D. Roles and family influences

7. A retailer sets very low prices on one or more items in its store to attract as many shoppers as possible, figuring that the lost revenue from these items will be offset by additional purchases of regular-priced merchandise.
   This is an example of   7.____

   A. leader pricing   B. odd-even pricing
   C. price leadership   D. bait pricing

8. An example of *line extension* is when a

   A. clockmaker changes the second hand movement from a ticking to a sweeping motion
   B. company that produces baking soda begins to promote the product as a deodorizer
   C. paper towel producer tries to acquire new customers by targeting organizational markets
   D. cola company develops a new lemon-lime flavored soft drink

9. An effective and useful market segmentation scheme should define segments that meet each of the following criteria EXCEPT

   A. undifferentiated response to marketing variables
   B. measurability
   C. size
   D. accessibility

10. Each of the following is a practice specifically forbidden by the provisions of the Robinson-Patman Act EXCEPT

    A. indefensible quantity discounts
    B. exclusive dealings and tying contracts
    C. fictitious brokerage
    D. disproportional supplementary services and allowances

11. Typically, which of the following elements would appear FIRST within an annual marketing plan?

    A. Current situation
    B. Executive summary
    C. Objectives
    D. Marketing strategy

12. Marketing efforts that are based on the information-search phase of the consumer decision-making process typically take each of the following factors into account EXCEPT

    A. total amount of information available to consumers
    B. relative importance of information sources
    C. percentage of the target market using specific information sources
    D. relative influence of family members

13. A consumer displays the following patterns of buying behavior: She purchases products such as insurance to achieve financial security, consumes consciously but cautiously, and typically purchases high-quality products in pursuit of gracious living. According to market conventions, this consumer most likely occupies the _____ class.

    A. upper
    B. upper-middle
    C. lower-middle
    D. upper-lower

14. In terms of security and defensibility, which of the following trademarks is ranked highest in the trademark hierarchy?

    A. Pacific Bell (telephone service)
    B. Kodak (film)
    C. Marion (laboratories)
    D. Escalator

15. Typically, most of a company's product lines are in the _____ stage of their respective life cycles at any given point in time.

    A. introductory or growth
    B. growth or shakeout
    C. growth or maturity
    D. maturity or decline

16. Legal protection for utility and design inventions is provided by a

    A. patent
    B. trademark
    C. copyright
    D. brand

17. Which of the following is NOT a step involved in the workload approach to establishing the size of a sales force?

    A. Determining how many customers are in each of a set of established categories
    B. Multiplying the number of potential customers in each category by the number of categories
    C. Estimating the number of calls a salesperson can make in one year
    D. Dividing the total number of calls that need to be made by the average number of calls a salesperson can make in a year

18. Which of the following factors, used to determine the buying power index (BPI) of a certain geographic area, is nost highly weighted?

    A. Retail sales
    B. Distribution
    C. Income
    D. Population

19. Each of the following is an example of supporting goods EXCEPT

    A. lubricants
    B. flour sold to bakeries
    C. cash register tape
    D. cleaning materials

20. Generally, one who manufactures, produces, or packages products may be held responsible to a person who suffers harn from the use of the product upon each of the following grounds EXCEPT

    A. assault
    B. breach of implied warranty of fitness
    C. negligence
    D. breach of express warranty

21. Which of the following marketing strategies is probably LEAST useful for a company that has adopted an *analyzes* position in a certain market?

    A. Encirclement
    B. Flanker strategy
    C. Leapfrog strategy
    D. Frontal attack

22. What is the term for market-research tests in which subjects are asked to perform tasks for specific purposes while they are in fact being evaluated for other purposes?

    A. Patronage motives
    B. Attitude scales
    C. Projective techniques
    D. Covert interviews

23. The practice of penetration pricing is likely to be used in the marketing of

    A. an older line of children's clothing
    B. food and beverage products
    C. a frequently stocked-out line of home appliances
    D. a new line of personal computers

24. The easiest, but still generally effective, method for determining absolute market potential is to base the potential on

    A. the buying power index
    B. estimates prepared and aggregated from information on the use opportunities presented by various segments
    C. current industry sales
    D. the competitive structure of the market

25. A company produces a liniment as a remedy for muscle pain due to bruises or overexertion, and distributes the product to retail supermarkets. If the company discovers a new use for the product, it would MOST likely

    A. promote the liniment as a means of warming up muscles before exercise
    B. simplify the product line
    C. begin to withdraw from the retail market and target professional sports teams
    D. modify the product slightly to widen its appeal

KEY (CORRECT ANSWERS)

1.	B		11.	B
2.	A		12.	A
3.	C		13.	B
4.	D		14.	B
5.	C		15.	D
6.	B		16.	A
7.	A		17.	B
8.	D		18.	C
9.	A		19.	B
10.	B		20.	A

21. D
22. C
23. B
24. C
25. A

TEST 4

DIRECTIONS: Each question or incomplete statement is followed by several suggested answers or completions. Select the one that BEST answers the question or completes the statement. *PRINT THE LETTER OF THE CORRECT ANSWER IN THE SPACE AT THE RIGHT.*

1. In setting physical distribution objectives, which of the following strategies is MOST likely to be adopted by a marketing-oriented company?

    A. Do everything possible to minimize physical distribution costs, and then establish a multi-channel system in which intermediaries can assume a large portion of service costs
    B. Establish a reasonable level of service that will keep customers happy, and do everything possible to minimize physical distribution costs of providing this level of service
    C. View service costs as variable, doing everything possible to ensure customer satisfaction, and look upon the increased costs of physical distribution as an investment in future expansion
    D. Focus entirely on the minimum total cost

2. As a promotional tool, personal selling is MOST significant in the marketing of _____ goods.

    A. durable
    B. convenience
    C. industrial
    D. specialty

3. A company that decides to produce a pocket calculator that is much like the calculator produced by a competitor will probably encounter each of the following EXCEPT

    A. relatively low R&D costs
    B. a relatively high market share
    C. a lowered risk
    D. an easier introductory period

4. In marketing a certain product, a business is pursuing a differentiated defender strategy, and competition for distribution support is strong.
Most likely, what is the company's most important personal selling objective?

    A. Maintaining customer loyalty
    B. Developing new customers
    C. Communicating product information
    D. Technical service to facilitate sales

5. Which of the following is NOT considered to be a benefit associated with the practice of target-return pricing? It

    A. can assist in estimations of market demand
    B. can be set at a rate that is considered both fair from a public policy standpoint and attainable from a company standpoint
    C. is relatively clear for internal company purposes
    D. can assure a company of meeting its financial objectives

6. Each of the following is a typical advantage associated with a retailer's use of a wholesaler's services EXCEPT

    A. wider product line
    B. efficient handling of customer service claims
    C. more efficient physical distribution activities
    D. coordination of supply sources

7. Which of the following is NOT a type of factor that appears to influence organizational buying decisions?

    A. Psychological
    B. Environmental
    C. Interpersonal
    D. Individual

8. Each of the following is a typical risk assumed by a franchisee EXCEPT

    A. overexpansion
    B. unproven track record of product
    C. scant marketing research
    D. poor management

9. A snack-food company wants to enter the market with a cookie featuring white chocolate chips and macadamia nuts. Marketing research has revealed that most customers wanted the maximum amount of white chocolate in their cookies, with only a small amount of nuts. The research department labels this group as segment Y. There were two other distinct segments revealed in the study: segment X (people who wanted a lot of nuts, and very little white chocolate) and segment Z (people who wanted small amounts of each). Segment X was the smallest segment.
    After this study, the company decides to target segment Z. The most likely reason for this is

    A. the company already produces a product that will satisfy segment Y
    B. unreliable research staff
    C. strong competition for the largest market segment
    D. high cost of ingredients

10. The authorization of the FTC and the Secretary of Health, Education, and Welfare to issue regulations to ensure truthful disclosure of producer identity and other relevant packaging practices was the major provision of the

    A. Federal Trade Commission Act
    B. Magnuson-Moss Warranty--Federal Trade Commission Improvements Act
    C. Fair Packaging and Labeling Law
    D. Food, Drug, and Cosmetics Act

11. The purpose of offering trade discounts is to

    A. permit low-income end-use customers to obtain necessary goods through the offer of unique services
    B. discourage the extension of credit to end-use customers
    C. provide an agent with a commission that does not come from the sales budget
    D. pay a wholesaler or retailer for the functions they form for a manufacturer

12. Which of the following types of sales promotion usually has the smallest impact on sales?   12._____

    A. Coupons
    B. Premiums
    C. Trading stamps
    D. Money refunds

13. Which of the following are examples of shopping goods?   13._____

    A. Stereo equipment
    B. Furniture
    C. Umbrellas
    D. Cameras

14. Which of the following market characteristics is MOST favorable for a frontal attack strategy on the part of a company entering the market?   14._____

    A. A relatively homogeneous market with respect to customer needs and purchase criteria; relatively little preference or loyalty for existing brands
    B. Two or more major segments with distinct needs and purchase criteria; the needs of customers in at least one segment not being met by existing brands
    C. Relatively heterogeneous market with a number of larger segments; needs and preferences of customers in most segments currently satisfied by competing brands
    D. Relatively homogeneous market, but some needs of criteria not currently met by existing brands

15. _____ marketing research questioning will offer a marketer the greatest control over the sample used.   15._____

    A. Personal at home
    B. Mail
    C. Personal at shopping center
    D. Telephone

16. _____ goods are characterized by maximum distribution, consumer advertising, and merchandising.   16._____

    A. Convenience
    B. Durable
    C. Shopping
    D. Novelty

17. Which of the following types of wholesalers is concerned mainly with facilitating exchange through selling activities?   17._____

    A. Specialty-line
    B. Truck wholesaler
    C. Drop shipper
    D. Limited-line

Questions 18-19.

DIRECTIONS: Questions 18 and 19 refer to the following information.

In a certain marketing channel network, a wholesaler's markup on a certain product is 20%, and the retailer's markup is 50%. The producer sells the product to a wholesaler for a price of $14.50.

18. For what price would the wholesaler sell the product to the retailer?   18._____

    A. $14.50   B. $17.40   C. $17.98   D. $21.75

19. What would the end-use customer end up paying for the product? 19.____

    A. $17.98 B. $21.75 C. $23.20 D. $26.10

20. An example of an institutional market is a(n) 20.____

    A. church purchasing hymnals
    B. employee of the Federal government buying household goods for her own home
    C. wholesaler buying syringes for resale to individual medical practitioners
    D. municipal government purchasing a water treatment system

21. The MOST important factor in an organizational user's selection of equipment is typically 21.____

    A. technical simplicity   B. price
    C. prestige   D. customer service

22. Which of the following is NOT a *disadvantage* associated with horizontal channel integration? 22.____

    A. Difficulty coordinating large number of units
    B. Increase in planning and research
    C. Purchasing inefficiency
    D. Decrease in flexibility

23. Which of the following is LEAST likely to function as a separate facilitating agency? 23.____

    A. Transportation
    B. Marketing research agency
    C. Buying center
    D. Insurance company

24. Generally, the most commonly experienced *exit barrier* to a company's disengagement from a business that is unprofitable is that 24.____

    A. the fixed assets involved have little liquidation value or high conversion costs
    B. management has an emotional tie to the business because of history or tradition
    C. national economic policy prevents some firms from exiting an industry
    D. higher management's sense of loyalty to employees

25. According to the marketing concept, which of the following characteristics does NOT describe a retail institution that has recently entered a market? 25.____

    A. Low-inventory   B. Low-status
    C. Low-margin   D. Low-price

KEY (CORRECT ANSWERS)

1. B
2. C
3. B
4. A
5. A

6. B
7. A
8. B
9. C
10. C

11. D
12. D
13. B
14. A
15. D

16. A
17. C
18. B
19. D
20. A

21. D
22. C
23. C
24. A
25. A

EXAMINATION SECTION
TEST 1

DIRECTIONS: Each question or incomplete statement is followed by several suggested answers or completions. Select the one that BEST answers the question or completes the statement. *PRINT THE LETTER OF THE CORRECT ANSWER IN THE SPACE AT THE RIGHT.*

1. When the United States made the transition from an agrarian to an industrial economy,
   I. the process of marketing became significantly more efficient
   II. education contributed by embarking upon more professional studies
   III. an expanded transportation system brought markets and sources of supply within the reach of urban centers
   IV. ecpnomic efforts were concentrated on providing the worker with the highest standard of living in the world
   V. new distribution techniques were established

   The CORRECT answer is:

   A. I, V B. II, III C. I, II
   D. I, II, IV, V E. All of the above

2. Which of the following customers are the manufacturer's top purchasers?
   I. Wholesalers
   II. Industrial users
   III. Manufacturers' branches
   IV. Ultimate consumers
   V. Foreign buyers

   The CORRECT answer is:

   A. I, IV B. I, II, V C. II, III
   D. II, III, V E. I, II, III

3. Why are agricultural marketing problems *more* complicated than those of manufacturing?
   I. Production is geographically concentrated
   II. The location is often unfavorable for marketing
   III. There is little control over the quality and quantity of output
   IV. The farmer specializes in a line of goods sold through a single marketing channel
   V. The national economy is no longer predominantly agrarian

   The CORRECT answer is:

   A. I, III, V B. I, II, III C. II, III
   D. III, IV, V, E. III, IV

4. What are the disadvantages of direct marketing?
   I. Contacts with consumers are not so close as they are under the direct supervision of a middleman
   II. Prices cannot be controlled as they can be with the middleman's facilities and marketing knowledge
   III. Investment is increased when the producer assumes the function of the middleman
   IV. The cost of sales and office personnel is increased
   V. Risks are increased

   The CORRECT answer is:

   A: I, II, V B. I, III, IV, V C. III, IV, V
   D. II, V E. All of the above

5. Which of the following are TRUE of standardization?
    I. It does not alter the physical make-up of the product
    II. Quantitative standards are most often used in marketing
    III. Farmers depend primarily on agricultural methods to meet standards of industry
    IV. It increases the risk factor particularly for producers marketing for the ultimate consumer's preferences
    V. It affects manufactured products far more than agricultural or the extracting industries' products
   The CORRECT answer is:

   A. I, II, V
   B. II, III, IV
   C. II, IV, V
   D. All of the above
   E. None of the above

6. Which of the following is(are) MOST LIKELY to use the services of the whoesaler?
    I. Small scale retailers
    II. Retailer groups
    III. Chain stores
    IV. Mail order houses
    V. Department stores
   The CORRECT answer is:

   A. I only
   B. I, II
   C. IV only
   D. III, V
   E. All of the above

7. Which of the following effects are TRUE of price fluctuation based on the marketing channel?
    I. Wholesaler prices are lower than retailer prices
    II. Retailer prices fluctuate more widely than wholesaler prices
    III. Wholesaler and retailer prices are subject to more abrupt price variations than producer prices
    IV. Retail prices are the least stable because of the low profit margin of operation
    V. Producer prices vary in response to changing conditions
   The CORRECT answer is:

   A. I, II, III, IV
   B. I, II, IV
   C. I, III, IV, V
   D. I, V
   E. All of the above

8. Which of the following are common types of discounts? _____ discounts.
    I. Quantity
    II. Anticipation
    III. Preference
    IV. Promotional
    V. Status
   The CORRECT answer is:

   A. I, II, IV
   B. I, III, IV, V
   C. I, IV, V
   D. I, III, IV
   E. All of the above

9. What are the results of storage of goods?
    I. Certain risks of ownership are reduced
    II. Transportation costs are reduced
    III. Greater fluctuations in prices are permitted
    IV. The prices of commodities are increased
    V. Waste of certain products is reduced or eliminated
   The CORRECT answer is:

   A. I, III, IV   B. II, V   C. I, II, V
   D. IV, V   E. All of the above

10. What are the disadvantages of short-term loans?
    I. The bank may place restrictions on them
    II. They are relatively expensive
    III. They are difficult to obtain
    IV. The purchaser often becomes dependent on market sources or channels
    V. They may encourage overspending
   The CORRECT answer is:

   A. I, II, III   B. I, V   C. I, III
   D. II, III, IV, V   E. All of the above

11. At the present stage of economic development, the United States must concern itself with
    I. improving its methods of distribution
    II. insufficient numbers of workers to meet productive requirements
    III. inadequate industrial capacity
    IV. establishing parity between the movement of products with production itself
    V. avoiding maladjustment between production and consumption through more efficient marketing
   The CORRECT answer is:

   A. I, II, IV, V   B. I, III   C. II, III, V
   D. I, IV, V   E. All of the above

12. What are the advantages of the local wholesaler in comparison with the national or regional wholesaler? The local wholesaler
    I. knows the customers personally
    II. can accurately judge credit risks
    III. is able to operate at low cost
    IV. is able to buy certain goods in sufficient quantities to obtain discounts
    V. is able to offer reduced costs because of less diversified stocks
   The CORRECT answer is:

   A. I, II   B. I, II, V   C. I, II, III
   D. I, II, IV, V   E. All of the above

13. The local wholesale market for agricultural products is similar to the secondary wholesale market in that *both*
    I. buy and sell agricultural products
    II. grade and standardize agricultural products for sale
    III. provide storage facilities
    IV. perform a financing function
    V. incur risks by taking physical possession of the goods
    The CORRECT answer is:

    A. I, IV
    B. II, III, IV, V
    C. I, IV, V
    D. I, III, IV, V
    E. All of the above

14. What are the requirements for direct marketing by personal solicitation? The
    I. product should be relatively small so that it is reasonably portable
    II. product should be one that is ordered in large quantities by the average customer
    III. producer should have adequate capital to maintain services in the chief market areas product should be relatively difficult to obtain through standard market outlets
    IV. product should lend itself to ready description
    The CORRECT answer is:

    A. I, II, IV
    B. II, III
    C. I, III, IV
    D. II, III, IV, V
    E. All of the above

15. What are the advantages of restricted distribution for the producer?
    I. Distribution costs are reduced
    II. The producers can concentrate on distribution and promotion through other channels
    III. The middleman adjusts prices to meet those of the competitors
    IV. The middleman's efforts for the producer's products are increased
    V. Exclusive sponsorship increases the product's prestige
    The CORRECT answer is:

    A. I, II, IV, V
    B. I, IV, V
    C. I, V
    D. III, IV, V
    E. II, III, IV, V

16. When there is, more or less, a regular pattern of change in supply and demand,
    I. "long-run normal prices" prevail
    II. cyclical fluctuations occur
    III. secular fluctuations occur
    IV. price changes occur in response to business cycles
    V. price fluctuation is minimized
    The CORRECT answer is:

    A. I *only*
    B. III, V
    C. II, IV
    D. All of the above
    E. None of the above

17. Which of the following are TRUE of discounts?
    I. Government restrictions have raised prices on purchases by large-scale retailers
    II. The proliferation of private brands has resulted in producers offering extra discounts to specific customers
    III. The scale of discounts must be related to the reduction of the costs of production
    IV. Functional discounts are offered in accordance with the buyer's position in the channel of distribution
    V. Most quantity discounts are cumulative to the wholesaler and non-cumulative to the retailer

    The CORRECT answer is:

    A. I, IV, V
    B. II, IV, V
    C. I, III, IV
    D. II, III, IV, V
    E. All of the above

18. Which of the following statements are TRUE of storage?
    I. Industrial goods are stored more often than non-industrial goods.
    II. When surpluses require storage, the gap between consumption and production is widened.
    III. Storage often improves the quality of commodities.
    IV. Storage encourages standardization of products.
    V. Storage makes goods more available to buyers.

    The CORRECT answer is:

    A. II, V
    B. III, IV, V
    C. I, II, IV, V
    D. I, II, V
    E. None of the above

19. Which of the following improvements of managerial methods will *reduce* risk?
    I. Producing only on order
    II. Careful grading, sorting, and standardization of commodities
    III. Specialization
    IV. Elimination of branding
    V. budgetary pT.anning

    The CORRECT answer is:

    A. I, II, III
    B. II, III, IV, V
    C. I, IV, V
    D. I, II, V
    E. All of the above

20. The *most commonly* used channel(s) of distribution for manufactured articles is(are) from producer
    I. to consumer
    II. to one middleman to consumer
    III. to wholesaler to retailer to consumer
    IV. through merchant middleman to wholesaler to retailer to consumer
    V. through agent middleman to wholesaler to retailer to consumer

    The CORRECT answer is:

    A. I *only*
    B. III *only*
    C. I, II
    D. IV *only*
    E. V *only*

21. The producer relies on the merchant wholesaler of consumer goods for
    I. the expense of selling the goods
    II. selling methods
    III. advice about packaging and size of units
    IV. lower freight sates
    V. extending credit to retailers
    The CORRECT answer is:

    A. I, II, IV
    B. I, IV
    C. IV, V
    D. I, III, IV, V
    E. All of the above

22. Which of the following types of middlemen buy *directly* from the farmer?
    I. Local buyers
    II. Representatives of the central market
    III. Domestic merchants
    IV. Local retailers
    V. Local jobbers
    The CORRECT answer is:

    A. I, V
    B. I, III, IV
    C. I, IV, V
    D. I, III, V
    E. All of the above

23. What are the advantages of Mail-Order Marketing?
    I. Products reach customers in scattered areas
    II. Contact with customers is direct
    III. It is inexpensive
    IV. It is an outlet for products the middleman is unwilling to stock
    V. Marketing is faster by mail
    The CORRECT answer is:

    A. I, III, IV
    B. I, II, V
    C. I, V
    D. I, II, IV, V
    E. All of the above

24. Which of the following items are generally sold *directly* to the manufacturer to the industrial consumer?
    I. Low-cost items
    II. Items of general use by business
    III. Raw materials
    IV. Specialized merchandise
    V. High-cost items
    The CORRECT answer is:

    A. I, II
    B. I, II, III
    C. III, IV
    D. III, IV, V
    E. IV, V

25. What are the advantages of restricted distribution for the middleman?
    I. Income is likely to be stabilized
    II. Less work is required because the volume of sales is restricted
    III. Increased independence results from exclusive contracts
    IV. Prestige is increased by association
    V. New products are easily introduced from an established producer
    The CORRECT answer is:

    A. I, II, III
    B. I, IV, V
    C. II, III
    D. IV, V
    E. All of the above

26. What factors cause price fluctuations?
    I. Supply of the product
    II. Marketing channels
    III. Size of the marketing area
    IV. Supplier's suggestions
    V. Mechanical aspects
    The CORRECT answer is:

    A. I, III, IV
    D. I, II, IV, V
    B. I, II, III
    E. All of the above
    C. I, IV

27. What are the differences between sales to wholesalers and to retailers? Wholesalers
    I. do not sell to the ultimate consumer
    II. are not particularly interested in the quality of a product
    III. generally buy from representatives of other groups of middlemen
    IV. carry a more highly specialized inventory
    V. sell merchandise in larger quantities
    The CORRECT answer is:

    A. I, IV, V
    D. III, IV, V
    B. I, II, V
    E. All of the above
    C. I, III, IV

28. What are the standards for good storage?
    I. Facilitate the collection of the government customs tax
    II. Inspection of goods
    III. Locations convenient for transportation
    IV. Monitoring "bonded" products
    V. Ability to provide all requested services
    The CORRECT answer is:

    A. II, III, V
    D. I, II, V
    B. III, V
    E. All of the above
    C. I, II, III, IV

29. How does horizontal integration *differ* from vertical integration? It helps to
    I. *control* more of the steps necessary for the production of a commodity
    II. *determine* wholesale and retail distribution
    III. *encourage* the operation of retail establishments
    IV. *process* more closely allied products
    V. *increase* capacity
    The CORRECT answer is:

    A. I, II, III
    D. II, III
    B. II, III, V
    E. All of the above
    C. IV, V

30. The "Functional Approach" to the study of marketing includes the
    I. process of concentrating or controlling goods or services with a transfer of title
    II. process of assisting a prospective customer to purchase a commodity that has commercial significance to the seller
    III. physical transferr of commodities from the place of production to the place of consumption
    IV. distribution of both industrial and consumer goods
    V. analysis of the agencies which do the marketing
    The CORRECT answer is:

    A. I, V
    D. All of the above
    B. III, IV
    E. None of the above
    C. I, II, III

31. What are the advantages of the Specialty Wholesaler over the Merchandise and General-line competitors? The Specialty Wholesaler
    I. specializes in a limited number of brands
    II. is a buying specialist
    III. has lower costs because his dealings are restricted to a single line
    IV. is able to meet the customer's demands because of his specialization
    V. buys in large quantities

    The CORRECT answer is:

    A. I, II, III B. I, II, IV C. II, V
    D. I, II E. All of the above

32. Which of the following *advantages* are TRUE of the Farm Cooperative?
    I. It makes for price stabilization by reducing the number of small lots being offered for sale competitively
    II. Profits are increased by its excellent business methods
    III. Unlike other markets, the Cooperative has the strength of a permanent and stable membership
    IV. It achieves more orderly marketing by controlling production
    V. It maintains a large and efficient sales organization for independent farmers

    The CORRECT answer is:

    A. I, V B. I, III, IV C. II, IV, V
    D. I, IV E. All of the above F.

33. Which of the following are TRUE of direct marketing by integration? The
    I. producer assumes the functions of the typical industrial market wholesaler
    II. product is one whose average sales are in large quantities
    III. product does not require specialized selling
    IV. product does not require installation skills
    V. market area must be sufficiently concentrated

    The CORRECT answer is:

    A. I, III, IV B. I, V C. I, III, IV, V
    D. I, II, V E. All of the above

34. What are the *advantages* of quantity buying?
    I. Items are generally discounted
    II. During periods of inflation, prices rise after purchase
    III. Stock is stabilized
    IV. Transportation costs are reduced
    V. It attracts customers

    The CORRECT answer is:

    A. I only B. I, III, V C. I, II
    D. I, II, IV E. All of the above

35. What are the *disadvantages* of Restricted Distribution for the middleman?
    I. Sales volume is decreased
    II. There is little assurance that the producer will continue the agreement
    III. Prestige is tied to the producer and the product
    IV. It is more difficult to meet competition
    V. More time and energy are expended by increased involvement in marketing trends and pricing
    The CORRECT answer is:

    A. I, II, III
    B. II, III, V
    C. II, III, IV
    D. I, II, III, V
    E. All of the above

36. Which of the following effects are TRUE of price fluctuations?
    I. When the demand for an item is elastic, changes in price do not result in sizable changes in sales
    II. During periods of recession, prices increase
    III. Supply and demand tend to become equal on a local rather than a regional or national basis
    IV. Smaller businesses often do not set prices according to their cost and net profits
    V. Suppliers' prices are dictated by the demands of wholesalers or retailers
    The CORRECT answer is:

    A. I, II, V
    B. II, V
    C. III, V
    D. III, IV
    E. All of the above

37. Which of the following statements are TRUE of warehouses?
    I. Public warehouses are privately owned but operation and fees may be regulated by the government.
    II. Field warehouses lease space to owners who wish to retain physical and legal control over their goods.
    III. Custom warehouses are for goods impounded by the government.
    IV. Internal Revenue warehouses act as government agents to collect taxes before the goods are marketed.
    V. Custodial warehouses are used exclusively for the storage of government property.
    The CORRECT answer is:

    A. I, III, IV, V
    B. I, III
    C. I, II
    D. III, IV, V
    E. I, II, III

38. Which of the following steps should proceed personal selling?
    I. Preparation of a budget
    II. Gathering of material
    III. Market analysis
    IV. Making up a "call sheet"
    V. Sales analysis
    The CORRECT answer is:

    A. I, II, IV
    B. II, IV, V
    C. II, IV
    D. III, IV
    E. All of the above

39. Which of the following conditions are necessary for a commodity to be traded on an exchange? The
    I. commodity must be homogeneous
    II. supply of the commodity must be copious
    III. commodity must attract the interest of a large number of producers and consumers
    IV. supply of the commodity must be dependable
    V. commodity must be available for large-scale sales throughout the year
   The CORRECT answer is:

   A. I, II, III B. I, II, V C. II, IV, V
   D. I, III, IV E. All of the above

40. Which of the following groups of purchasers represent the consumer market?
    I. Producers
    II. Service organizations
    III. Institutions
    IV. Government
    V. Middlemen
   The CORRECT answer is:

   A. I, II, V B. II, III, , IV C. III, IV
   D. All of the above E. None of the above

41. Which of the following limited-function wholesalers are the least successful in terms of relations with manufacturers or retailers? The
    I. cash-and-carry wholesaler
    II. drop shipper
    III. truck wholesaler
    IV. mailer-order wholesaler
    V. retailer-wholesaler
   The CORRECT answer is:

   A. I, IV B. II, III, IV C. I, II, III
   D. IV, V E. II, III

42. How does the central warehouse market differ from the local wholesale market? It
    I. is more specialized than the local market
    II. does not perform all the marketing functions of the local market
    III. is situated in a center of transportation
    IV. sells to the large industrial consumers
    V. re-grades the commodities from the local markets
   The CORRECT answer is:

   A. I, II, III, IV B. I, III, V C. III, IV, V
   D. I, II, III E. All of the above

43. Which of the following is (are) a type(s) of door-to-door selling? When
    I. the producerr places his stock along the street
    II. the farmer operates a vegetable stand
    III. service organizations call and pick up on regular routes
    IV. the prospective customer requests a demonstration or a salesman [to call on him
    V. a sales representative attempts to market by personal solicitation
    The CORRECT answer is:

    A. V only   B. I, II, III   C. IV, V
    D. III, IV, V   E. I, III, IV, V

44. When a purchaser buys the total quantity of goods required and stores them for future use, it is called buying.
    I. anticipation
    II. forward
    III. advance
    IV. contract
    V. control
    The CORRECT answer is:

    A. I, II   B. III only   C. V only   D. IV, V   E. II, III

45. The producer is usually unable to dictate prices for his products when goods are
    I. resold in grocery outlets
    II. resold in drug outlets
    III. resold in chain stores
    IV. resold by mail order houses
    V. specialty items
    The CORRECT answer is:

    A. I, II, III   B. III, IV   C. II, IV, V
    D. All of the above   E. None of the above

46. What are the arguments *against* price maintenance? It
    I. *subsidizes* the inefficient retailer
    II. *increases* the use of private brands
    III. *augments* the manufacturer's profits at the expense of the retailers
    IV. *prevents* the consumer from underestimating the value of the product
    V. *emphasizes* none-price competition
    The CORRECT answer is:

    A. I, IV   B. I, II   C. II, III, V   D. II, V   E. II, IV

47. The salesman engaged in personal selling must have
    I. knowledge of the use, care, advantages, and disadvantages of the product
    II. knowledge of the competitor's products
    III. the ability to judge the prospect's reaction during the selling process
    IV. mastered the techniques of salesmanship
    V. samples available for inspection
    The CORRECT answer is:

    A. I, IV   B. I, II   C. I, IV, V
    D. I, II, III, IV   E. All of the above

48. What are the effects of transportation? Transportation
    I. strongle influences the location of markets
    II. affects marketing costs
    III. determines marketing schedules
    IV. affects the market for certain goods
    V. affects consumer demand for particular items
    The CORRECT answer is:

    A. II, IV, V   B. III, IV   C. I, II
    D. III, IV, V   E. II, III, IV

49. Which of the following statements are TRUE of speculation on a commodity exchange? It
    I. *provicdes* protection against losses from price changes
    II. *decreases* marketing costs because operators require less margin
    III. increases the effectiveness of competition since one needs less capital in order to enter the field
    IV. *encourages* loans
    V. *raises* prices paid to producers
    The CORRECT answer is:

    A. IV, V   B. I, II, V   C. II, III, V
    D. All of the above   E. None of the above

50. How are the characteristics of the industrial market *different from* those of a consumer market?
    I. There are a limited number of purchasers
    II. There is a geographic concentration of purchasers
    III. Most purchases stem from expediency or other considerations then performance
    IV. There is a greater frequency of purchase
    V. Buying responsibility is diffused
    The CORRECT answer is:

    A. II, IV, V   B. II, III, IV, V   C. IV, V
    D. I, V   E. All of the above

KEY (CORRECT ANSWERS)

1. B	11. D	21. D	31. C	41. B
2. E	12. C	22. B	32. A	42. C
3. C	13. D	23. A	33. D	43. E
4. C	14. B	24. E	34. D	44. B
5. E	15. B	25. D	35. A	45. B
6. A	16. E	26. A	36. D	46. B
7. D	17. C	27. B	37. B	47. D
8. A	18. B	28. A	38. D	48. C
9. C	19. D	29. C	39. A	49. E
10. A	20. B	30. C	40. E	50. D

EXAMINATION SECTION
TEST 1

DIRECTIONS: Each question or incomplete statement is followed by several suggested answers or completions. Select the one that BEST answers the question or completes the statement. *PRINT THE LETTER OF THE CORRECT ANSWER IN THE SPACE AT THE RIGHT.*

1. *How* does the merchant wholesaler of industrial goods differ from the merchant wholesaler of consumer goods in terms of services offered? The industrial wholesaler
   - I. assists in selling
   - II. offers rapid transportation at low cost
   - III. is able to store large quantities of stock
   - IV. is able to extend credit
   - V. is able to provide market information

   The CORRECT answer is:

   A. I, III, V   B. III, IV, V   C. III, IV
   D. All of the above   E. None of the above

   1.____

2. *How* does the jobber market differ from the mill market in agricultural distribution? It
   - I. does not take title to the goods
   - II. distributes industrial goods
   - III. exists for agricultural goods without change in form
   - IV. is run by wholesalers who are concentrated in factory towns
   - V. is far less common than the mill market

   The CORRECT answer is:

   A. I, II, IV   B. III, IV   C. II, III, IV, V
   D. All of the above   E. None of the above

   2.____

3. *What* are the *principal* advantages of house-to-house selling? It
   - I. is helpful to producers wishing to introduce new products
   - II. is useful when articles require home demonstration
   - III. offers more flexibility than marketing through a middleman
   - IV. lends itself to rural areas where public transportation is inadequate or non-existent
   - V. requires little supervision and little capital to maintain the sales force

   The CORRECT answer is:

   A. I, II, IV   B. II, IV, V   C. I, II, III
   D. II, IV   E. All of the above

   3.____

4. Profits *usually* depend upon:
   - I. Skill in purchasing
   - II. Thorough knowledge of the market in which the trading is done
   - III. Brilliant promotional advertising
   - IV. Maintaining an adequate inventory
   - V. Buying large quantities during a deflationary period and small quantities during an inflationary period

   The CORRECT answer is:

   A. I, II, IV   B. I, II, III, V   C. I, II, V
   D. I, II, IV, V   E. All of the above

   4.____

5. In economic theory, the "long-run normal price" results when
    I. the highest profitable volume of distribution has been achieved
    II. the costs of production and distribution have been reduced to an absolute minimum
    III. supply and demand are equalized for standard items
    IV. there is insufficient demand for a new product
    V. there is optimum use of production facilities
   The CORRECT answer is:

   A. I, III
   B. III, IV
   C. I, II, V
   D. I, II, IV
   E. All of the above

6. What are the advantages of pricing through the technique of price lining? It
    I. *helps* the firm's buyer evaluate the cost price of the
    II. merchandise
    III. *broadens* the market of the business enterprise
    IV. *simplifies* the selection problems of the customer
    V. *is easier* to maintain price lines for commodities subject to price fluctuations
    VI. *simplifies* making adjustments in lines during times of rising or falling prices
   The CORRECT answer is:

   A. I, III, V
   B. II, IV, V
   C. I, II, III
   D. III, IV, V
   E. All of the above

7. What are the important reactions a salesman should strive to obtain from the buyer during personal selling?
    I. Getting attention
    II. Product identification
    III. Stimulating desire
    IV. Dynamic response
    V. Obtaining action
   The CORRECT answer is:

   A. I, III, V
   B. I, IV, V
   C. I, II, V
   D. I, V
   E. All of the above

8. Which of the following types of marketing research studies are *correctly* identified?
    I. A market study desfribes the size and other characteristics of the market
    II. A marketing study determines consumer preference for special brands of commodities
    III. An economic study relates broad economic and social trends to problems of distribution
    IV. A news and information study describes establishing proper distribution channels
    V. A product study supplies data about prices, market conditions, and the like
   The CORRECT answer is:

   A. I, II
   B. II, III, V
   C. I, III, V
   D. III, IV, V
   E. I, III

9. Which of the following constitute advantages of the commodity exchange? It
    I. *leads to* standardization and grading
    II. *eliminates* the need of owners of goods to carry surplus stocks until they are required
    III. *prohibits* or *reduces* the practice of arbitrage
    IV. *encourages* the collection and dissemination of market news
    V. *aids* producers to. cope with price changes
   The CORRECT answer is:

   A. I, II, IV
   B. I, IV
   C. I, III, IV
   D. I, II, IV, V
   E. All of the above

10. Why have consumer cooperatives been slow to grow in the United States?
    I. Membership is usually limited
    II. Control is hierarchical
    III. Americans enjoy a high standard of living
    IV. Effective low-cost retailing is present in the economy
    V. Membership fees are required
    The CORRECT answer is:

    A. I, III, V
    B. I, II, III
    C. III, IV
    D. II, III, IV, V
    E. All of the above

11. Which of the following agent middlemen have greater opportunity to engage in unfair practices? The
    I. commission merchant
    II. selling agent broker
    III. purchasing agent
    IV. manufacturer's agent
    The CORRECT answer is:

    A. I, II   B. I, III, V   C. II, III   D. IV, V   E. I, III

12. Which of the following economic changes have led to the development and success of large-scale retailing?
    I. Growth of suburban areas
    II. Use of advertising to stimulate consumer interest
    III. Willingness of the customer to travel long distances to central stores
    IV. Increased variety of goods
    V. Higher salaries in inflationary periods
    The CORRECT answer is:

    A. I, II, III, IV
    B. II, III, V
    C. I, II, IV
    D. All of the above
    E. None of the above

13. When farmers directly market their agricultural products, they
    I. must have a location close to prospective customers
    II. avoid normal marketing expenses
    III. are able to retail commodities that fall below standardized grading specifications
    IV. obtain higher prices than available through middlemen
    V. do not require the established clientele of the middleman.
    The CORRECT answer is:

A. I, II, III, IV	B. I, IV	C. I, III
D. II, III, V	E. II, IV, V	

14. Producers are able to eliminate the services of a middleman when
    I. sales involve style goods
    II. perishable agricultural commodities are involved
    III. dealing with processed perishable agricultural goods
    IV. the item is of low unit value
    V. products with mechanical parts require installation and servicing
    The CORRECT answer is:

A. I, II, IV	B. III, V	C. I, II
D. I, III, IV, V	E. All of the above	

15. *How* do economists account for the disequilibrium in the supply and demand of products in the United States?
    I. Surplus and scarcity of products is unpredictable
    II. New production processes may emerge at any time
    III. High overhead costs often cause producers to rapidly disappear from the marketing scene
    IV. Depressions in the economy cause rapid turnovers among producers entering or leaving the marketing scene
    V. Labor groups negotiating new contracts or conducting strikes affect supply and demand
    The CORRECT answer is:

A. I, II, IV	B. I, IV, V	C. I, III, IV, V
D. I, II, V	E. All of the above	

16. *How* are sellers influenced by consumer habits and preferences in determining the price of their products?
    I. Pricing reflects consumer demand of particular items
    II. Prices of certain items are based upon custom or convenience
    III. Prices are often set below the nearest dollar value
    IV. Purchases involving larger sums are usually negotiated between buyer and seller
    V. Prices are frequently based on use
    The CORRECT answer is:

A. I, III	B. I, III, IV	C. IV, V
D. I, II, III	E. All of the above	

17. *What* are the *major* results of advertising? It
    I. *increases* the quantity of consumer purchases
    II. *decreases* the variety of consumer purchases
    III. *confuses* the consumer when attempting to differentiate among branded products
    IV. *stimulates* demand
    V. *helps raise* the standard of living
    The CORRECT answer is:

A. I, II, III, IV	B. I, II	C. I, IV, V
D. All of the above	E. None of the above	

18. What does an "Accounting Study" include?
    I. Measurement of economic trends
    II. Interpretation of available economic data
    III. Analyses of sales
    IV. Investigation of the costs of various distribution channels
    V. Research into the budgeted cost of each marketing function
    The CORRECT answer is:

    A. I, II, III
    D. I, III, IV, V
    B. II, III
    E. All of the above
    C. IV, V

18.____

19. What are the *major* disadvantages of the commodity exchange? It
    I. *permits* destructive transactions to be completed by
    II. inexperienced or dishonest speculators
    III. *subjects* prices to artificial conditions
    IV. *allows* the unscrupulous manipulation of prices
    V. *increases* fluctuations in prices
    VI. *makes* financing more difficult
    The CORRECT answer is:

    A. I, II, III
    D. I, III
    B. II, IV, V
    E. All of the above
    C. II, III, V

19.____

20. What are the *major* principles of the consumer cooperative?
    I. Limited rate of interest on capital
    II. Sale of goods at current market prices
    III. Available credit
    IV. Limited membership
    V. Patronage dividends
    The CORRECT answer is:

    A. I, III, V
    D. I, II, V
    B. III, V
    E. All of the above
    C. III, IV, V

20.____

21. Long-term contracts are common among
    I. brokers
    II. commission merchants
    III. manufacturer's agents
    IV. selling agents
    V. purchasing agents
    The CORRECT answer is:

    A. I, IV
    D. I, II
    B. III, V
    E. All of the above
    C. III, IV, V

21.____

22. Which of the following characterizations are TRUE of chain stores?
    I. They discount items
    II. Location is rarely significant
    III. Advertising is relatively inexpensive
    IV. Merchandising is flexible enough to meet varied location requirements
    V. Customer services are minimized to ensure low prices
    The CORRECT answer is:

22.____

| A. I, III, V | B. I, II, IV | C. I, V |
| D. II, IV | E. All of the above | |

23. What are the *advantages of* direct marketing through the producers' retail stores?
    I. The cost of distribution is decreased
    II. Retail stores of this type have wide appeal and sell to a broader area than the ordinary channels
    III. There is closer customer contact
    IV. The selling process is more easily controlled
    V. Products can be sold that middlemen or ordinary retailers would not stock
    The CORRECT answer is:

| A. I, II, III | B. I, IV, V | C. I, II, IV |
| D. III, IV, V | E. All of the above | |

24. Which of the following goods require the use of the complete marketing channel?
    I. Shopping and specialty goods
    II. Industrial goods
    III. Goods that represent a high sales volume
    IV. Goods that have a wide distribution
    V. Seasonal goods
    The CORRECT answer is:

| A. I, V | B. II, III, IV | C. IV, V |
| D. All of the above | E. None of the above | |

25. Which of the following features are TRUE of pure competition?
    I. The idea assumes a constant, uniform supply of products
    II. All products for sale are identical from the purchaser's point of view
    III. Prices are established by tradition
    IV. The seller has no influence upon price
    V. Sellers increase their income by advertising or other means of sales promotion
    The CORRECT answer is:

| A. I, II | B. III, IV, V | C. II, IV |
| D. All of the above | E. None of the above | |

26. Which of the following are advantages of a one price policy? It
    I. *reduces* competition
    II. *builds* good will for the seller
    III. *saves* time for both buyer and seller
    IV. *diminishes* the power of the buyer to dictate prices
    V. *tends* to result in lower selling prices with increased volume of sales
    The CORRECT answer is:

| A. I, III, V | B. II, III, IV | C. I, II, III, V |
| D. I, III | E. All of the above | |

27. *Which* of the following kinds of media are used more for industrial selling than consumer selling?
    I. Magazines and newspapers
    II. Outdoor displays
    III. Radio and television
    IV. Directories and catalogs
    V. Special menus and programs
    The CORRECT answer is:

    A. IV, V
    B. II, IV, V
    C. I, II, IV
    D. II, V
    E. None of the above

28. *Which* of the following statements are TRUE of marketing research?
    I. It is most beneficial to the small businessman.
    II. Formal reports are usually too data-conscious to be practically useful to large companies.
    III. Information often serves the researcher's needs, not the businessman's.
    IV. It may decrease the accuracy of an executive's judgment.
    V. Properly used, it is a substitute for experience and training.
    The CORRECT answer is:

    A. I, V
    B. I, II, IV
    C. II, III, IV
    D. All of the above
    E. None of the above

29. *Which* of the following are the *most common* devices used by businessmen to shift risk?
    I. Averaging risks
    II. Holding sales
    III. Inserting an escalator clause in contracts
    IV. Speculating on inventory for small profits
    V. Hedging
    The CORRECT answer is:

    A. II, III, V
    B. II, III, IV
    C. I, II, III
    D. All of the above
    E. None of the above

30. *What* are the *principal* reasons for the formation of consumer cooperatives?
    I. The costs of distribution are excessively high
    II. Business groups ignore consumer interests
    III. Government regulations increase the cost of goods
    IV. Labor unions ignore consumer interests
    V. Selling and advertising are often detrimental to consumer interests
    The CORRECT answer is:

    A. I, III, V
    B. I, II, V
    C. II, III, IV, V
    D. II, III, IV
    E. All of the above

31. *Which of* the following agent middlemen have freedom in arranging prices and sales conditions?
    I. Brokers
    II. Commission merchants
    III. Manufacturer's agents
    IV. Selling agents
    V. Purchasing agents
    The CORRECT answer is:

A. I, IV, V   B. IV, V   C. II, IV
D. All of the above E. None of the above

32. *What* are the *major* activities of the department store?
    I. Publicity
    II. Transportation
    III. Production
    IV. Merchandising
    V. Finance
    The CORRECT answer is:

    A. I, IV   B. II, III, IV, V   C. I, II, III, IV
    D. I, IV, V   E. IV, V

33. *How* do state laws discriminate against buying and selling activities? By
    I. heavily taxing businesses incorporated in other states
    II. restricting the shipment of certain products
    III. placing heavy taxes on products competing with a state's manor industries
    IV. imposing fees and regulations designed to hamper interstate trucking
    V. instituting restrictive controls over marketing practices
    The CORRECT answer is:

    A. I, II   B. III, IV, V   C. II, III, IV
    D. III, IV   E. All of the above

34. *Which* of the following considerations are *vital* to the selection of a middleman? The
    I. kind of middleman
    II. adequacy of the middleman's facilities
    III. middleman's ability to distribute the product
    IV. middleman's location
    V. middleman's attitude toward the product and the producer
    The CORRECT answer is:

    A. I, II, IV   B. I, III, IV   C. II, III, V
    D. II, III, IV   E. III, V

35. *Which* of the following observations are TRUE of a monopoly?
    I. Theoretically, it is the opposite of pure competition although very similar in practice
    II. Its existence depends on the public need for the commodity
    III. It monopolizes the marketing channels through an exclusive method of distribution
    IV. Price fixing depends on the availability of substitute products
    V. Price fixing depends on the purchases of a few large-column buyers
    The CORRECT answer is:

    A. I, III, IV   B. II, IV   C. I, II
    D. II, V   E. II, III, IV, V

36. Price leadership is found where
   I. there are relatively few producers
   II. highly specialized goods are marketed
   III. goods are widely advertised
   IV. there are high, fixed operating expenses
   V. there is a fairly constant turnover of companies entering and leaving the market

   The CORRECT answer is:

   A. I, III, IV
   B. II, IV, V
   C. I, II, III
   D. II, V
   E. All of the above

37. Direct selling copy
   I. establishes favorable public attitudes toward a product
   II. describes the organization's policies
   III. explains the distribution of profits
   IV. develops good public relations
   V. delimns the range and benefits of the work force

   The CORRECT answer is:

   A. I, IV, V
   B. I, II, IV
   C. II, III, V
   D. All of the above
   E. None of the above

38. "Marketing Financing" refers to the provision
   I. and management of funds needed to finance the carrying of stocks
   II. and management of funds needed to grant mercantile and retail credit
   III. and management of funds needed for installment credit
   IV. of funds to purchase a building in which to carry on a marketing enterprise
   V. of funds needed for consumer borrowing on a personal basis

   The CORRECT answer is:

   A. I, II, IV
   B. I, IV
   C. II, III, V
   D. I, II, V
   E. All of the above

39. Which of the following characterizations are TRUE of agent middlemen?
   I. They negotiate purchases or sales or both
   II. They perform most or all of the distributive functions
   III. The chief type of agent middleman is the wholesaler
   IV. They usually do not take title to the goods
   V. They receive remuneration in the form of commission or fee

   The CORRECT answer is:

   A. I, V
   B. I, II, IV
   C. I, IV, V
   D. All of the above
   E. None of the above

40. What are the differences between retailing middlemen and wholesaling middlemen? The
   I. retailing middleman completes the marketing process
   II. number of retailing middlemen exceeds that of wholesaling middlemen
   III. sales volume of retailing middlemen exceeds that of wholesaling middlemen
   IV. retailing middlemen act as agents in buying merchandise for, or selling merchandise to, institutional and professional users
   V. retailing middlemen are the major customers of the wholesaling middlemen

   The CORRECT answer is:

| A. I, II, V | B. I, II, III | C. III, IV |
| D. All of the above | E. None of the above | |

41. *Which* agent middlemen resemble commission merchants in activity but receive their profits from sellers?
    I. Brokers
    II. Manufacturer's agents
    III. Resident buyers
    IV. Purchasing agents
    V. Selling agents
    The CORRECT answer is:

    | A. I, IV, V | B. II, IV, V | C. I, V |
    | D. II, III | E. III, IV | |

42. Direct marketing is *most feasible* when
    I. the goods to be sold are standard or are traditional items with established customers
    II. the producer concentrates on a single product
    III. service requirements are minimal
    IV. competition is minimal
    V. the middlemen, during periods of recession, refuse to maintain maximum resale prices
    The CORRECT answer is:

    | A. I, III, V | B. II, IV, V | C. I, III |
    | D. All of the above | E. None of the above | |

43. *What* are the results of diversification of product line?
    I. Customer satisfaction
    II. Elimination of unprofitable operations
    III. Commodity prices are lowered
    IV. The danger of a product being "out of stock" is minimized
    V. Capital required for inventory is increased
    The CORRECT answer is:

    | A. I, V | B. I, II, III | C. I, III, IV |
    | D. All of the above | E. None of the above | |

44. *Which* of the following are TRUE statements?
    I. The elimination of the middleman generally reduces distribution costs.
    II. Most industrial goods are distributed to the industrial consumer market via middlemen.
    III. The smaller the average sale to the ultimate consumer, the less chance there is for direct selling.
    IV. Distribution facilities which function only part of the year are ineffective for all but seasonal products.
    V. Most priducers utilize the channels of distribution used by their competitors.
    The CORRECT answer is:

    | A. I, II, IV | B. II, III, IV | C. I, III, IV |
    | D. III, V | E. All of the above | |

45. *Which* of the following types of competition are prevalent in the American economy?
    I. Pure competition
    II. Free competition
    III. Monopoly
    IV. Imperfect competition
    V. Semi-monopoly
    The CORRECT answer is:

    A. I, II   B. II, IV   C. IV, V   D. II, III, IV   E. II, IV, V

46. *Which* of the following factors made it possible for middlemen to play a more substantial role in the economy?
    I. National expansion
    II. Spread of the media
    III. Development of new products
    IV. Growth of sectionalism
    V. Expansion of the labor force
    The CORRECT answer is:

    A. I, V
    D. II, III, V
    B. I, IV
    E. All of the above
    C. I, III, IV

47. *Which* of the following methods is(are) categorized as "personal selling?"
    I. Door-to-door salesmen
    II. Advertising campaigns
    III. Media publicity
    IV. Vending machines
    V. Retail stores
    The CORRECT answer is:

    A. I, IV   B. I only   C. I, IV, V   D. I, V   E. I, II, III, V

48. *Which* of the following factors affect both the time and amount of mercantile credit?
    I. Rate of stock turnover
    II. Availability of transportation
    III. Value of the commodity
    IV. Nature of the commodity
    V. Income period of the buyer
    The CORRECT answer is:

    A. I, V
    D. I, II, IV, V
    B. I, II, V
    E. All of the above
    C. III, IV, V

49. In *what* areas do marketing functions differ from merchandising?
    I. Selecting the articles to be produced
    II. Packaging
    III. The quantities to be bought or made
    IV. The time of purchase
    V. Price lines to be made or carried
    The CORRECT answer is:

    A. I, IV
    D. All of the above
    B. II, III, IV
    E. None of the above
    C. II, IV, V

50. Which of the following are *major* characteristics of business buying?
     I. Prompt delivery is more significant than price or performance
     II. Business demands depend on consumer demands
     III. Buying decisions are made by very few designated officers
     IV. Businesses rarely feel obligated to engage in reciprocal buying
     V. All buying is the result of laboratory tests or other investigations
   The CORRECT answer is:

   A. I, III, IV
   B. II, III, IV
   C. I, II
   D. II, III, V
   E. None of the above

KEY (CORRECT ANSWERS)

1. E	11. A	21. C	31. C	41. E
2. B	12. C	22. A	32. D	42. E
3. C	13. B	23. D	33. E	43. A
4. A	14. C	24. C	34. E	44. D
5. C	15. D	25. C	35. B	45. C
6. C	16. D	26. B	36. A	46. C
7. A	17. C	27. A	37. E	47. D
8. E	18. C	28. E	38. D	48. D
9. B	19. D	29. C	39. A	49. A
10. C	20. D	30. B	40. A	50. C

EXAMINATION SECTION
TEST 1

DIRECTIONS: Each question or incomplete statement is followed by several suggested answers or completions. Select the one that BEST answers the question or completes the statement. *PRINT THE LETTER OF THE CORRECT ANSWER IN THE SPACE AT THE RIGHT.*

1. PRODUCTION refers to the
    I. division of the total product of industry among the factors of land, labor, capital, and management
    II. utilization of the products of industry
    III. creation of utility
    IV. change of form which occurs in the factory, farm, forest, fishery, or mine
    V. creation of place, time, and possession utilities
   The CORRECT answer is:

   A. I, III   B. I, V   C. II, V   D. I, IV   E. III, IV

   1._____

2. How does *grading* differ from *dividing*? Goods are
    I. separated into smaller lots
    II. separated to meet the needs of the buyers
    III. separated on the basis of quality
    IV. separated on the basis of quantity
    V. inspected and tested
   The CORRECT answer is:

   A. I, II, III   B. III, V   C. II, V
   D. IV, V   E. All of the above

   2._____

3. The transportation function of marketing includes the movement of
    I. raw materials from producer to producer
    II. partly manufactured goods within the factory
    III. raw materials within the mine
    IV. parts and sub-assemblies within the warehouse
    V. finished goods from producer to consumer
   The CORRECT answer is:

   A. I, II, III, IV   B. II, III, IV   C. I, III
   D. I, V   E. II, IV

   3._____

4. *Which* of the following are TRUE of goods moved by rail?
    I. When goods are shipped in carlot shipments, the railroads load and unload the goods
    II. When goods are shipped in carlot shipments, the railroad usually picks up and delivers them to the receiver
    III. Of the total number of tons of freight moved, the greater part is moved in less than carlot shipments
    IV. Most of the freight revenue is made up of goods shipped by carlots
    V. The rate per 100 lbs. is ordinarily lower on less-than-carlot shipments than on carlot shipments

   4._____

The CORRECT answer is:

A. I, II, V B. IV, V C. III, IV, V
D. III, V E. None of the above

5. Which of the following are true of warehouse receipts?
   I. Negotiable receipts are more flexible than non-negotiable receipts
   II. Most bank loans on inventories are loaned on non-negotiable receipts
   III. Negotiable receipts do not have to leave the holder's possession for release of part of the lot If a non-negotiable receipt is lost, the goods cannot be obtained without posting a bond
   IV. Negotiable receipts are frequently used when the whole lot of goods will be withdrawn as a block

   The CORRECT answer is:

   A. I, III, 7 B. I, IV C. II, IV, V D. II, V E. I, II, IV, V

6. Economists consider exchange. as including a(n)
   I. *place* where goods are offered for sale
   II. *place* where buyers and sellers meet
   III. *area* within which price-determining factors operate
   IV. *area* where there is a demand for goods
   V. *meeting* of people for buying and selling

   The CORRECT answer is:

   A. I, II, V B. II, III, IV C. III, IV
   D. All of the above E. None of the above

7. *Which* of the following are TRUE of storing? It
   I. creates time utility creates place utility
   II. refers to necessary wrapping and crating of goods
   III. is one of the more important and expensive marketing activities
   IV. is a function of physical movement

   The CORRECT answer is:

   A. I, V B. II, IV, V C. II, III
   D. All of the above E. None of the above

8. *How* is *packaging* different from packing? Packaging
   I. generally means placing of goods in small packages
   II. is meant for sale to ultimate consumers
   III. is one of the most expensive parts of the marketing process
   IV. increases the salability of goods
   V. allows the seller to obtain higher prices than those obtained for similar goods sold in bulk

   The CORRECT answer is:

   A. III, IV, V B. I, III, V C. I, II, IV, V
   D. II *only* E. All of the above

9. *What* are the advantages of the railroad over truck transportation?
   I. Railroads deliver goods in less time
   II. Goods do not require so much packing
   III. Rates are commonly lower
   IV. Better service is available for heavy or bulky goods
   V. Railroads reach wider markets

   The CORRECT answer is:

   A. I, IV, V
   B. II, IV, V
   C. IV, V
   D. III, IV
   E. All of the above

10. *What* are the disadvantages of using public warehouses?
    I. It spreads the goods out geographically
    II. Damage or loss is increased
    III. Transportation costs are increased
    IV. Taxes are increased
    V. It is expensive especially for seasonally produced goods

    The CORRECT answer is:

    A. I, II, III
    B. II, III, V
    C. I, IV
    D. All of the above
    E. None of the above

11. The area or size of the market is *most directly* increased by
    I. marketing techniques
    II. improvements in transportation
    III. increase in the population
    IV. increase in the population's income level
    V. increase in the quantity of goods

    The CORRECT answer is:

    A. I, III, IV
    B. I, IV, V
    C. II, III, IV
    D. III, IV, V
    E. All of the above

12. How does the merchant determine his needs? By
    I. studying sales records
    II. fashion trends
    III. habit
    IV. customer preferences
    V. displays and advertisements of competing goods

    The CORRECT answer is:

    A. I, II, IV
    B. I, III
    C. I, V
    D. I, IV, V
    E. All of the above

13. In wholesale houses, *order picking* means
    I. the order in which goods are shipped
    II. the order in which goods are assembled
    III. getting goods together for delivery
    IV. delivery of items to the shipping platform
    V. loading and unloading goods from trucks or railroad cars

    The CORRECT answer is:

    A. I, IV
    B. III, IV
    C. II, III, IV, V
    D. II, III, IV
    E. None of the above

14. What advantages do trucks have over transportation by rail? Trucks
    I. enable shippers to transport smaller quantities
    II. shorten trade channels
    III. are more dependable
    IV. are better suited for bulky goods
    V. are better suited for moving livestock
    The CORRECT answer is:

    A. I, III   B. I, II, IV   C. I, II, V   D. I, IV, V   E. I, II

15. Which of the following services are performed by public merchandise warehouses?
    I. Goods are received in carlots, unloaded, and placed in storage
    II. Goods are packed for delivery
    III. Goods are sold to local buyers
    IV. Credit authorization is obtained
    V. Goods are delivered to buyers
    The CORRECT answer is:

    A. I only   B. I, II, V   C. II, III, IV, V   D. III, IV   E. I, II, III, V

16. Business is capable of almost indefinite expansion because
    I. a demand can be created for almost any product or service
    II. the incentive for profits is unlimited
    III. the population continues to expand
    IV. human wants are almost unlimited
    V. of the unlimited time people have for consumption
    The CORRECT answer is:

    A. I, II   B. IV only   C. III only
    D. III, IV, V   E. None of the above

17. What are the techniques used in price negotiation?
    I. Bids and offers
    II. Hedging
    III. Auctions
    IV. Promises and threats
    V. Fear
    The CORRECT answer is:

    A. I, II, III   B. I, IV   C. I, III, IV   D. IV, V   E. I, II, IV, V

18. What is the descending order of movement of freight within the United States?
    I. Pipe
    II. Rail
    III. III Waterways
    IV. Air
    V. Road
    The CORRECT answer is:

    A. IV, II, V, III, I   B. IV, V, II, I, III   C. II, V, IV, I, III
    D. V, IV, II, I, III   E. V, II, IV, III, I

19. *What* are the disadvantages of transportation by truck?
    I. Uncertain road conditions cause them to be unreliable
    II. There is considerable damage to goods
    III. Trucks often make for uncertain markets
    IV. Trucks often hurt the business of regularly established sellers by flooding the market with poor goods
    V. Trucks are a hazard on the public highways
    The CORRECT answer is:

    A. I, II, IV, V   B. I, II, III, V   C. I, II, V
    D. I, III, IV, V   E. All of the above

20. *What* do public warehouses charge for?
    I. Space used for the time the goods are stored
    II. Warehouse receipts
    III. Utilities
    IV. Taxes
    V. Handling
    The CORRECT answer is:

    A. I, V   B. I *only*   C. I, II   D. I, III, V   E. I, III, IV, V

21. *Which* of the following are TRUE of marketing costs?
    I. When commodity prices are risiing, marketing costs decrease relatively
    II. When commodity prices are falling, marketing costs increase
    III. When prices are rising, marketing takes a higher percentage of the final selling price
    IV. When prices are falling, a lower percentage of the final selling price is taken
    V. Marketing prices usually change more quickly than the prices of commodities
    The CORRECT answer is:

    A. I, II   B. III, IV   C. I, II, V
    D. III, IV, V   E. All of the aboove

22. *Why* do sellers give advice and assistance to buyers? To
    I. keep customers satisfied
    II. increase sales
    III. justify price increases
    IV. determine what the buyer should purchase
    V. promote less salable items
    The CORRECT answer is:

    A. I, II, III   B. I, II, III, V   C. I, II, V
    D. I, IV   E. All of the above

23. The railroads' physical plant consists of
    I. the sidings
    II. freight stations
    III. transfer houses
    IV. classification yards
    V. mechanical equipment
    The CORRECT answer is:

A. I, III	B. II, III, IV	C. I, II, III
D. II, IV, V	E. All of the above

24. *What* are the advantages of owner-operated trucks? Owners
    I. are able to adjust damage claims
    II. are able to combine delivery and sales services
    III. can secure the trucker's profits
    IV. eliminate the time spent negotiating with labor unions
    V. are able to formulate more accurate delivery schedules
    The CORRECT answer is:

    A. I, II, IV, V   B. II, III, V   C. II, V
    D. All of the above E. None of the above

25. When borrowing on inventories, the
    I. warehouse receipt is usually the most practical method
    II. warehouse receipt can only be issued by a reputable field warehouse
    III. goods must be stored in buildings owned and operated as field warehouses
    IV. lender must store goods used for chattel mortgages
    V. owner must store goods used for trust receipts
    The CORRECT answer is:

    A. I, III, V   B. I, II, V   C. I, IV
    D. All of the above E. None of the above

26. *What* are the distinguishing characteristics of industrial goods? They are
    I. used in carrying on industrial activities
    II. used in carrying on institutional enterprises
    III. used in a form without further commercial processing
    IV. not destined for ultimate consumption
    V. goods whose form has been changed for use by the ultimate consumer
    The CORRECT answer is:

    A. I, II   B. IV only   C. I, II, III, IV   D. I, III   E. I, II, V

27. Which of the following are TRUE of business risks?
    I. The greater the estimated hazard, the greater the anticipated profits
    II. When the risk is widely scattered, it should be shifted to insurance companies
    III. A large part of the risk of price changes can be shifted to others
    IV. When the risks cannot be lessened, goods can be marketed more cheaply
    V. When the risks can be eliminated or shifted, the smaller are the prospective profits necessary to attract capital
    The CORRECT answer is:

    A. I, II, IV   B. II, IV, V   C. I, III, V
    D. III, V   E. All of the above

28. Which of the following are TRUE of carriers?
      I. Goods are transferred by their owners by common carriers
      II. Contract carriers operate over specified routes
      III. Common carriers move goods between points specified by the owners
      IV. Public carriers transport goods or people for pay
      V. Most goods are transported by agent carriers
   The CORRECT answer is:

   A. I, III, IV   B. II, III, IV   C. II, IV, V
   D. IV, V   E. II, III, IV, V

29. The system of distribution used by an individual company varies with the
      I. kind of product involved
      II. number of products involved
      III. size of the company
      IV. territory covered by the company
      V. company's inventory of products
   The CORRECT answer is:

   A. I, II, IV   B. II, V   C. I, IV, V
   D. III, IV   E. All of the above

30. What regulations govern field warehouses? The
      I. owner must have access to the stored goods
      II. lease must be recorded in the courthouse
      III. lease must include a full legal description
      IV. custodian of the goods must be bonded
      V. owner must carry legal liability bonds indemnifying holders of receipts against loss resulting from failure of the warehouseman to discharge his duties properly
   The CORRECT answer is:

   A. I, II, III, V   B. II, III, V   C. I, V
   D. II, III, IV, V   E. All of the above

31. What is a manufacturers' agent? An agent who
      I. operates on an extended contractual basis
      II. sells within an exclusive territory
      III. handles noncompeting but related goods
      IV. has limited authority with regard to prices
      V. determines the terms of the sale
   The CORRECT answer is:

   A. I, II   B. II, IV, V   C. I, II, III, IV
   D. II, III   E. All of the above

32. Marketing-management is directly concerned with:
      I. Negotiating
      II. Formulating policies
      III. Financing
      IV. Transferring title
      V. Providing organization and equipment
   The CORRECT answer is:

A. I, II, V	B. II, III, V	C. II, V
D. I, II, IV, V	E. All of the above	

33. Which of the following are TRUE of liability?
    I. When the common carrier refuses to carry up to the limit of his capacity, it may render him liable for damages
    II. Only acts of nature relieve the carrier of the responsibility for the safe delivery of goods
    III. The carrier is liable only as a warehouseman and not as a carrier upon arrival at the terminal destination
    IV. A demurrage is involved when cars are held too long for loading or unloading
    V. When the receiver does not remove goods within a reasonable time, the carrier is liable for loss only in the case of his negligence
    The CORRECT answer is:

    A. I, III
    B. II, III, IV
    C. I, II, III
    D. II, IV, V
    E. All of the above

34. What are the advantages of regional warehouses?
    I. Accounting is simplified
    II. Goods reach the warehouses much more quickly
    III. Field salesmen are eliminated
    IV. Inventories are increased for both the manufacturer and the wholesaler
    V. Damage from stale goods and spoilage is reduced
    The CORRECT answer is:

    A. II, III, IV
    B. I, III, IV
    C. I, II, V
    D. I, II
    E. All of the above

35. What are the factors that determine the location of warehouses?
    I. Transportation costs
    II. Cost of land in the area
    III. Cost of labor in the area
    IV. Population of the area
    V. Standard of living in the area
    The CORRECT answer is:

    A. I, IV
    B. II, III, IV
    C. I, II, III
    D. II, III, V
    E. I, II, III, V

36. Which of the following are sales personnel employed by the manufacturer to create goodwill among customers?
    I. Manufacturers' agents
    II. Marketing facilitating agents
    III. Missionary salesmen
    IV. Detailers
    V. Sellers' agents
    The CORRECT answer is:

    A. I, II, V
    B. III, IV
    C. II, IV
    D. I, V
    E. II, III, IV

37. When a bill of lading is a *straight bill,* it
    I. is a negotiable bill
    II. carries title to the goods
    III. can be used as collateral for loans
    IV. is used when the shipper wants to receive payment for the goods before they pass into the buyer's hands
    V. is commonly used in the sale of commodities
    The CORRECT answer is:

    A. I, V
    B. I, II, IV
    C. II, III, IV
    D. All of the above
    E. None of the above

38. The marketing function of creating possession utility includes:
    I. Determining needs
    II. Financing
    III. Transportation
    IV. Accounting
    V. Transferring title
    The CORRECT answer is:

    A. I, III, V
    B. II, IV, V
    C. II, III, IV, V
    D. I, III
    E. I, V

39. *Why* is storage necessary?
    I. Goods are not produced regularly at the place of consumption
    II. Raw materials are needed at the place of production
    III. It reduces the costs of transportation
    IV. The demand for some products is irregular
    V. It increases customer satisfaction
    The CORRECT answer is:

    A. I, II, IV
    B. I, II
    C. I, III, IV
    D. I, III, V
    E. I, II, IV, V

40. *What* are the disadvantages of one-story warehouses?
    I. Reserve stock cannot be stored clearly separated from active stock
    II. Time and money are wasted by workers having to cover large expanses of floor space
    III. Construction costs are higher
    IV. It is cheaper to move goods vertically than horizontally
    V. Operation is more expensive
    The CORRECT answer is:

    A. I, II, V
    B. II, III, IV, V
    C. III, IV
    D. All of the above
    E. None of the above

41. Goods are purchased by:
    I. Policy
    II. Inspection
    III. Grade
    IV. Value
    V. Description
    The CORRECT answer is:

    A. I, II, V
    B. II, IV
    C. I, II, IV
    D. II, III, V
    E. All of the above

42. The marketing function of creating place and time utility includes:
    I. Order assembly
    II. Finding buyers and sellers
    III. Creating or stimulating demand
    IV. Transportation
    V. Adjusting goods and services to the needs of the buyers
    The CORRECT answer is:

    A. I, IV   B. II, III, IV, V   C. I, II, III
    D. II, III, V   E. IV *only*

43. Transit privileges
    I. allow certain commodities to be removed and reloaded at a later time
    II. often determine the location of industries
    III. allow a car to be reassigned to another location upon arrival
    IV. provide for changes in destination before arrival
    V. help the shipper to avoid additional local rate charges
    The CORRECT answer is:

    A. I, II   B. I, III, IV   C. III, IV, V
    D. All of the above E. None of the above

44. Which of the following are TRUE of public warehouses?
    I. The warehouseman has custody of the goods stored
    II. They operate to store other peoples' goods for pay
    III. The warehouseman is as fully liable as the common carrier
    IV. In a rising market more of the goods are owned by sellers
    V. In a falling market, more of the goods are owned by buyers
    The CORRECT answer is:

    A. II, IV, V   B. I, II   C. IV, V
    D. II, III   E. All of the above

45. Which of the following are TRUE? A household
    I. consists of more people than a family
    II. consists of a family with children
    III. is made up of all the people occupying a dwelling unit
    IV. includes both related and unrelated individuals
    V. is the common buying unit
    The CORRECT answer is:

    A. I, II, III   B. I, V   C. I, III, IV, V   D. III, IV, V   E. I, III

46. Business policy determines:
    I. Quality and variety of goods to be sold
    II. Manner of sale
    III. Selling price
    IV. Extension of credit
    V. Manner of collection
    The CORRECT answer is:

    A. I, III, IV   B. II, V   C. III, IV, V
    D. I, II, III   E. All of the above

47. Which of the following are TRUE of distribution?
    I. It is only concerned with getting goods from the central markets to the consumers
    II. Commission merchants are involved primarily in dispensing goods and supplying them to customers
    III. Concentration and dispersion processes involve many of the same operations
    IV. Wholesalers are involved in dispersing goods and supplying them to their customers
    V. Concentration and dispersion activities come together at the central market
    The CORRECT answer is:

    A. I, V   B. I, III, IV   C. I, II, III   D. I, III, V   E. III, IV, V

48. What are the MAIN types of public warehouses?
    I. Merchandise
    II. Household goods
    III. Special commodity
    IV. Cold storage
    V. Field warehouses
    The CORRECT answer is:

    A. I, III, IV   B. I, II, III   C. IV, V
    D. I, III   E. All of the above

49. Which of the following are TRUE of railroad rates?
    I. Commodity rates are special or lower rates which apply to specified commodities shipped between any points in the country
    II. Commodity rates apply to both carload and less-than-carload shipments
    III. Commodity rates usually apply only to heavy commodities
    IV. Class rates apply to both carload and less-than-carloadshipments
    V. Class rates apply to the movement of commodities between specified points or areas
    The CORRECT answer is:

    A. I, II   B. II, IV, V   C. III, IV
    D. All of the above   E. None of the above

50. Studies of income indicate that as a family's income increases, it spends
    I. a smaller propoertion of it on food
    II. a higher proportion for rent and utilities
    III. a higher proportion for clothing
    IV. a lower amount for education
    V. approximately the same proportion on religion
    The CORRECT answer is:

    A. I, III, V   B. I, II, III   C. I, III, IV
    D. II, III, V   E. III, IV, V

KEY (CORRECT ANSWERS)

1. E	11. C	21. D	31. C	41. D
2. B	12. A	22. D	32. B	42. A
3. D	13. B	23. E	33. E	43. A
4. B	14. C	24. B	34. C	44. B
5. D	15. B	25. C	35. C	45. D
6. E	16. B	26. A	36. B	46. E
7. A	17. C	27. C	37. E	47. E
8. C	18. D	28. D	38. E	48. E
9. D	19. D	29. A	39. E	49. C
10. E	20. A	30. D	40. E	50. B

EXAMINATION SECTION
TEST 1

DIRECTIONS: Each question or incomplete statement is followed by several suggested answers or completions. Select the one that BEST answers the question or completes the statement. *PRINT THE LETTER OF THE CORRECT ANSWER IN THE SPACE AT THE RIGHT.*

1. *Which of* the following statements are TRUE?
    I. Place utility is created when goods are available at the places where they are needed.
    II. Time utility is created when goods are present at the time they are needed.
    III. Possession utility is created when goods are transferred to those who need them.
    IV. Production utility is created with the utilization of the products of industry.
    V. Form utility is created when goods are available in the form in which they are needed.
   The CORRECT answer is:

   A. I, II, III   B. I, II, V   C. III, V   D. I, II, III, V
   E. III, IV, V

2. *Why* are imports subject to tariffs?
    I. For control of foreign exchange
    II. For revenue
    III. To keep out foreign goods
    IV. To give domestic producers an advantage
    V. To reduce our dependence on foreign trade
   The CORRECT answer is:

   A. I, II, III   B. III, IV, V   C. I, II, III, IV
   D. II, III, IV   E. All of the above

3. *Which* of the following statements are TRUE of buying and selling?
    I. The primary purpose of newspapers want ads is to find buyers.
    II. Retailers do much less active selling than wholesellers.
    III. In our economy, it is usually the buyer who seeks the seller.
    IV. Retailers secure much of their business from people who are familiar with their stores.
    V. Consumer buying is often compromised by limited available merchandise.
   The CORRECT answer is:

   A. I, IV, V   B. II, V   C. III, V   D. II, IV, V
   E. All of the above

4. The most competitively priced goods are _____ goods.
    I. convenience
    II. shopping
    III. specialty
    IV. impulse
    V. emergency
   The CORRECT answer is:

   A. I, II   B. I, II, III   C. I, IV   D. II, III, V
   E. II, IV, V

1.____

2.____

3.____

4.____

5. *Which* of the following are the *most common* causes of new product failures?
   I. Unexpected high product cost
   II. Company politics
   III. Product lacked meaningful uniqueness
   IV. Poor planning
   V. Product lacked a champion
   The CORRECT answer is:

   A. I, IV   B. I, III, V   C. I, III, IV   D. III, IV
   E. II, III, IV, V

6. *Which* of the following statements are TRUE of the costs of production and marketing?
   I. The cost of marketing has been steadily increasing.
   II. When goods are marketed near the point of production, marketing costs decrease.
   III. Marketing and production costs usually have the same rate of increase.
   IV. Marketing costs usually change more slowly than the prices of commodities.
   V. Labor-saving devices have generally helped lower marketing cqsts.
   The CORRECT answer is:

   A. I, II, IV   B. I, II, III   C. II, V   D. IV, V   E. I, III

7. *Which* of the following statements are TRUE of international trade?
   I. Nations become less and less dependent upon the importation of foreign goods as they become more highly industrialized.
   II. The exchange of raw materials for manufactured products is one of the most important basês of trade.
   III. Exchange controls are used to control barter deals.
   IV. Unlike domestic trade, international trade is more likely to be on a cash rather than on a credit basis.
   V. Marketing research agencies in foreign countries are better equipped to handle international trade than those in the United States.
   The CORRECT answer is:

   A. I, II, V   B. I, II, III   C. II, III, IV   D. II, III, IV, V
   E. All of the above

8. *Which* of the following are ways in which the ultimate consumer generally purchases goods?
   I. Inspection
   II. Sample
   III. Description
   IV. Grade
   V. Advice
   The CORRECT answer is:

   A. I, II, V   B. I, II, III   C. I, III, V   D. II, IV
   E. I, II, IV

9. Which of the following categories of goods are *not* dependent upon pricing for sales? _____ goods.
    I. Convenience
    II. Heterogeneous
    III. Specialty
    IV. Impulse
    V. Emergency

    The CORRECT answer is:

    A. I, III, V
    B. I, II, III, V
    C. I, V
    D. III, V
    E. II, III, V

9.____

10. *What* are the advantages of manufacturer's branded merchandise?
    I. It encousages repeat sales
    II. Retailers are more eager to handle branded merchandise
    III. Branded merchandise usually maintains its price in a falling market
    IV. Advertising and sales promotion is less expensive for branded merchandise.
    V. New products have more of a chance for acceptance if they are introduced under an established brand

    The CORRECT answer is:

    A. I, III, V
    B. II, III
    C. I, III, IV
    D. II, III, IV
    E. All of the above

10.____

11. Which of the following are arguments in favor of an increase in marketing costs? Increased marketing costs
    I. are an insurance against monopolies
    II. help to maintain prices of goods
    III. are necessary to place new products in the hands of consumers
    IV. reduce the number of unemployed and increase the standard of living
    V. help decrease production costs

    The CORRECT answer is:

    A. I, III
    B. I, II, III
    C. I, III, V
    D. II, III, IV
    E. III, IV, V

11.____

12. What are the *principal differences* between international and domestic interregional trade? The
    I. uniformity in commercial practices
    II. absence of exchange controls
    III. lack of trade regulations
    IV. movement of industry to decentralize
    V. method of marketing goods

    The CORRECT answer is:

    A. I, II, V
    B. I, II, III
    C. II, III, IV
    D. II, III, IV, V
    E. All of the above

12.____

13. The marketing division is DIRECTLY responsible for
    I. selling
    II. production
    III. transportation
    IV. accounting
    V. promotion
    The CORRECT answer is:

    A. I, II, III B. I, III, V C. I, III, IV, V D. I, III, IV
    E. All of the above

14. Which of the following is(are) example(s) of *shopping goods*?
    I. Grocery products
    II. Furniture
    III. Appliances
    IV. Stereo components
    V. Collector items
    The CORRECT answer is:

    A. I only B. II, III, IV, V C. II, V D. II, III
    E. II, IV, V

15. What are the *disadvantages* of private brands?
    I. They require quality control at a manufacturing factory not owned by the distributor
    II. The promotion necessary to achieve customer acceptance is very costly
    III. It is very difficult for a customer to compare private-branded merchandise with competitors' goods
    IV. Private brands are tailored *only* to the tastes of the dealer's specific customers
    V. The material and manufacturing cost is often so high that a competitive product cannot be offered
    The CORRECT answer is:

    A. I, III, V B. II, IV C. I, II, V D. II, III, IV
    E. I, III, IV

16. Wastes in marketing are *primarily* due to
    I. poor management
    II. unavoidable existing conditions
    III. lack of competition
    IV. creation of monopolies
    V. government regulations
    The CORRECT answer is:

    A. I, V B. I, II C. II, V D. I, III E. III, IV, V

17. What determines the location of wholesale houses?
    I. Power
    II. Labor
    III. Population
    IV. Transportation
    V. Service facilities
    The CORRECT answer is:

    A. I, II, III B. II, III, IV C. I, IV, V D. I, II, III, V
    E. IV, V

18. Which of the following factors must be blended together to achieve marketing success?   18._____
    I. Product
    II. Place
    III. Population
    IV. Price
    V. Ownership
    The CORRECT answer is:

    A. I, IV, V   B. III, IV, V   C. II, III   D. I, II, III, IV
    E. All of the above

19. Location is relatively *unimportant* for selling _____ goods.   19._____
    I. convenience
    II. shopping
    III. specialty
    IV. impulse
    V. emergency
    The CORRECT answer is:

    A. I, IV, V   B. I, IV   C. III, V   D. II, III
    E. II, III, V

20. What are the *advantages* of a franchise to the parent community?   20._____
    I. The amount of capital ordinarily needed to expand is reduced
    II. Unit managers operate more efficiently and profitably when their own capital is involved
    III. Overhead is reduced
    IV. Expansion is achieved without decreasing company ownership
    V. Outlets have more of a chance for success when they are owned by a resident of the community
    The CORRECT answer is:

    A. I, II, V   B. I, II, IV, V   C. II, III, IV, V   D. I, II, IV
    E. All of the above

21. The seller considers   21._____
    I. income statistics to be more important than population figures
    II. the number of people to be more important than the number of households
    III. national income to be one of the most widely used figures in marketing research
    IV. disposable income to be more important than discretionary buying power
    V. the consumer's location to be as important as his buying power
    The CORRECT answer is:

    A. I, II, III   B. I, III, V   C. II, III, IV   D. I, III, IV
    E. I, III

22. Which of the following statements are TRUE of retail trade movement?
    I. The movement of trade is from larger to smaller towns.
    II. High-income families buy more goods in town than do low income families.
    III. Towns attract trade in proportion to their size.
    IV. As travel time increases, trade flow decreases
    V. Weather conditions affect local sales.
    The CORRECT answer is:

    A. II, III, IV, V   B. I, II, III, IV   C. III, IV, V
    D. I, III, IV, V   E. All of the above

23. Which of the following evaluations are TRUE of *reciprocity* in the industrial market?
    I. Economic conditions are responsible for an increased use of reciprocity
    II. Reciprocity motivates product diversification
    III. Reciprocity is advantageous when new products are introduced for sale
    IV. Purchasing agents prefer reciprocity in simplifying purchasing procedures
    V. Reciprocity has the long-range effect of reducing prices
    The CORRECT answer is:

    A. I, II, III   B. I, IV, V   C. II, III   D. III, IV, V
    E. II, III, IV, V

24. Which of the following items are examples of *heterogeneous goods*?
    I. Furniture
    II. Appliances
    III. Automobiles
    IV. Television sets
    V. famous-brand clothing
    The CORRECT answer is:

    A. I, II, IV   B. I, II, III   C. II, V   D. I, V   E. I, III, V

25. Which of the following are *most important* in selecting a channel of distribution? The
    I. characteristics of the goods
    II. consumer market
    III. producer's and the retailer's locations
    IV. amount and type of competition
    V. financial strength of the producer
    The CORRECT answer is:

    A. I, V   B. I, II, IV   C. I, III   D. I, IV   E. I, II

26. On what basis, do consumers select sellers?
    I. Reputation
    II. Location
    III. Price
    IV. Services
    V. Selection
    The CORRECT answer is:

    A. I, IV   B. I, III, IV   C. I, II, III, IV   D. III, IV
    E. All of the above

27. What kinds of *motion* are part of the marketing function?
    I. Physical movement of goods
    II. Shifting risk
    III. Processing operations
    IV. Timing
    V. Change of ownership
    The CORRECT answer is:

    A. I, V   B. I, III, IV   C. II, V   D. I, III, IV, V
    E. All of the above

28. *What* are the advantages of leasing industrial equipment to the lessee?
    I. Smaller financial investment
    II. Total income distributed under a leasing arrangement is greater than that from an outright purchase
    III. Leasing offers an excellent method of distributing new, untried products
    IV. Obsolete equipment &s more readily traded-in
    V. Income tax savings involved with rentals are higher than the depreciation deduction for ownership
    The CORRECT answer is:

    A. I, II, III   B. I, IV, V   C. II, III, V   D. I, III, V
    E. III, V

29. Which of the following industrial goods are *rarely* sold through middlemen?
    I. Fabricating materials and parts
    II. Installations
    III. Services
    IV. Supplies
    V. Accessory equipment
    The CORRECT answer is:

    A. I, II, III   B. I, V   C. II, III   D. I, IV, V
    E. II, III, V

30. How do retailers *differ*, from wholesalers?
    I. They sell goods to ultimate consumers
    II. They buy in significantly larger quantities than wholesalers
    III. Their location is more important than for wholesalers
    IV. Their trading area is larger than that of wholesalers
    V. They are charged a higher price for manufacturer's goods than are wholesalers
    The CORRECT answer is:

    A. I, II, III   B. I, III, IV   C. I, IV, V   D. I, III, V
    E. All of the above

31. *Which* of the following are of prime *importance* in determining attitudes toward work?
    I. Land formation
    II. Ideology
    III. Government system
    IV. Philosophy
    V. Religion
    The CORRECT answer is:

    A. I, II, III   B. I, III, V   C. II, IV, V   D. I, III, IV, V
    E. II, III, IV, V

32. Transportation costs are high because
    I. of regional specialization of production
    II. of specialization of workers
    III. the units which are most efficient for the movement of goods are not exactly matched with the units of purchase or sale
    IV. of the distance between points of priduction and consumption
    V. of loading and unloading operations
    The CORRECT answer is:

    A. II, IV, V   B. IV, V   C. I, III, IV, V   D. III, V
    E. All of the above

33. *What* are the problems of leasing from the lessor's point of view?
    I. Enormous amounts of capital are required
    II. The risks of obsolescence are not spread out among many users
    III. The total income from a piece of equipment under a leasing arrangement is less than that from an outright sale
    IV. The opportunity for outright sales is diminished
    V. There is little opportunity to diversify or to introduce new products
    The CORRECT answer is:

    A. I, II   B. I, III   C. I, IV, V   D. I, III, V
    E. I, III, IV, V

34. *Which* of the following industrial goods are produced to the customer's specifications and marketed through short channels of distribution?
    I. Accessory equipment
    II. Installations
    III. Supplies
    IV. Fabricated materials
    V. Raw materials
    The CORRECT answer is:

    A. I, II, IV   B. I, III, IV   C. II, IV   D. IV, V   E. II, IV, V

35. Which of the following are *limited function wholesalers*?
    I. Cash and carry wholesalers
    II. Drop shippers
    III. Rack jobbers
    IV. General merchandise wholesalers
    V. Specialty wholesalers

A. I, III, V   B. I, II, III   C. II, III, IV   D. III, V
E. I, II, V

36. Which of the following MOST affect the occupations of people?
    I. Population density
    II. Geography
    III. Capital
    IV. Trade
    V. Economy
    The CORRECT answer is:

    A. I, II   B. II, III, IV, V   C. II, IV, V   D. III, IV, V
    E. I, IV, V

37. Why is stockkeeping important to the wholesaler and the retail merchant? It
    I. aids in the display of their goods
    II. *encourages* keeping complete and well-assorted stocks
    III. *helps* reduce or eliminate spoilage
    IV. *guards* against obsolescence
    V. *creates* time utility for seasonal goods
    The CORRECT answer is:

    A. II, V   B. I, II, III, IV   C. II, III, IV, V   D. I, II, V
    E. All of the above

38. How do industrial promotions differ from consumer goods promotion?
    I. Advertising is more -rational than emotional in its appeal
    II. Direct mail is favored over mass selling
    III. The size of the market rules out the use of the media
    IV. Advertising is carried on with the expectation of a sale
    V. Promotion of service and supply is more important than product advertising
    The CORRECT answer is:

    A. I, II, III   B. I, IV, V   C. I, IV   D. I, II, V
    E. I, II, IV

39. Which of the following reasons account for the United States' *unfavorable balance* of trade? Some
    I. increase in both the cost and the domestic use of oil
    II. foreign competitors produce more cheaply than we do
    III. foreign competitors have surpassed our technical know-how
    IV. foreign governments subsidize exporters
    V. foreign competitors are more innovative and better able to satisfy customer demand
    The CORRECT answer is:

    A. I, II   B. I, II, IV   C. I, III, IV   D. I, III, IV
    E. All of the above

40. What advantages does newspaper advertising have over the other media?
    I. Advertisements are usually seen by every member of the family
    II. Items for sale can be presented more attractively
    III. The life of the advertisement is longer
    IV. The cost per reader is lower
    V. Shorter distances from stores encourage readers to shop for advertised merchandise

    The CORRECT answer is:

    A. I, III, V   B. III, V   C. II, III, V   D. I, III
    E. All of the above

41. Which of the following reasons *justify* protective tariffs?
    I. Protection of infant industries
    II. National defense considerations
    III. Protection against an unfavorable balance of trade
    IV. The law of comparative costs
    V. The existence of *dumping*

    The CORRECT answer is

    A. I, III, IV   B. I, III, V   C. I, III   D. I, II, V
    E. All of the above

42. Which of the following are TRUE of *dividing*? It
    I. means separating goods into both the lot size and the quality required by the buyers
    II. is typically the function of manufacturers and wholesalers
    III. involves the actual work of separating goods according to previously established standards
    IV. is necessary for goods produced on a large scale and consumed on a small scale
    V. is not the most expensive of the marketing functions

    The CORRECT answer is:

    A. I, II, III   B. I, III, IV   C. IV, V   D. II, III, IV
    E. All of the above

43. Which of the following are TRUE of the industrial market?
    I. Price has little effect on the demand for industrial goods
    II. The demand for industrial goods fluctuates widely with general business conditions
    III. Industrial goods are usually bought from a middleman
    IV. The most important facifojbr in the distribution of industrial goods is personal selling
    V. Price is not dependent upon demand or business activity

    The CORRECT answer is:

    A. I, V   B. I, II, III   C. II, III   D. I, II, IV
    E. II, III, IV

44. Which of the following foreign-trade operations involve little or no risk?
    I. Foreign agents
    II. Company-owned sales branches
    III. Licensing
    IV. Joint ventures
    V. Wholly-owned subsidiaries
    The CORRECT answer is:

    A. I, III   B. II, V   C. I, III, IV   D. II, IV, V
    E. III, V

45. Which of the following statements are TRUE of advertising? It is
    I. not free
    II. non-personal stimulation
    III. a visual presentation of the goods to be sold
    IV. a form of publicity
    V. generally carried on through the mass media
    The CORRECT answer is

    A. I, II, V   B. I, V   C. III, IV, V   D. II, III, IV, V
    E. All of the above

46. Which of the following conditions are considered to be the basis of international trade?
    The inability of a country to
    I. *keep* all its labor employed in the most profitable industry if its population keeps increasing
    II. *produce* certain products
    III. *manufacture* a good for less than it costs to buy from another country
    IV. *develop* goods for national defense
    V. *satisfy* its capital loans
    The CORRECT answer is:

    A. I, II   B. II, III   C. II, IV   D. I, II, IV, V
    E. II, III, IV, V

47. Manufacturers and merchants secure market information from
    I. their salesmen
    II. fashion changes
    III. business conditions I
    IV. sales records
    V. forecasts of national income
    The CORRECT answer is:

    A. I, III, IV, V   B. I, IV, V   C. III, IV, V   D. I, IV
    E. All of the above

48. What are the characteristics of convenience goods?
    I. Goods are non-durable
    II. Brand is unimportant
    III. Goods are not expensive
    IV. Goods are bought by habit
    V. A large sales force is not required
    The CORRECT answer is:

A. I, II, III   B. I, III, IV   C. I, II, III, IV   D. I, II, IV, V
E. All of the above

49. Which of the following major channels of distribution available to United States exporters are listed in the order of their complexity and cost?
    I. Manufacturer - U.S. exporter-foreign importer-foreign wholesaler-foreign consumer
    II. Manufacturer-foreign wholesaler-foreign consumer
    III. Manufacturer-foreign consumer
    IV. Manufacturer-foreign importer based in the U.S.-foreign wholesaler-foreign consumer
    V. Manufacturer-foreign importer-foreign wholesaler-foreign consumer
The CORRECT answer is:

A. II, III, IV, V, I   B. III, II, IV, V, I
C. I, V, IV, II, III   D. III, II, V, IV, I
E. I, IV, V, II, III

50. Which of the following are examples of advertising?
    I. Novelties
    II. Direct mail
    III. Motion pictures
    IV. Demonstrations
    V. Shows
The CORRECT answer is:

A. II, IV   B. I, II, III   C. III, IV, V
D. I, II
E. I, III, IV, V

KEY (CORRECT ANSWERS)

1.	A	11.	C	21.	B	31.	C	41.	D
2.	D	12.	A	22.	C	32.	D	42.	C
3.	A	13.	B	23.	A	33.	A	43.	D
4.	C	14.	D	24.	E	34.	C	44.	A
5.	D	15.	C	25.	A	35.	B	45.	A
6.	D	16.	B	26.	E	36.	A	46.	B
7.	A	17.	E	27.	A	37.	B	47.	E
8.	C	18.	D	28.	B	38.	D	48.	B
9.	E	19.	C	29.	A	39.	E	49.	E
10.	A	20.	C	30.	D	40.	D	50.	B

EXAMINATION SECTION
TEST 1

DIRECTIONS: Each question or incomplete statement is followed by several suggested answers or completions. Select the one that BEST answers the question or completes the statement. *PRINT THE LETTER OF THE CORRECT ANSWER IN THE SPACE AT THE RIGHT.*

1. Which of the following is NOT a factor of production? 1.____

   A. Land
   B. Natural resources
   C. Promotion
   D. Capital

2. Country A has been growing wheat and corn for centuries to supply its own citizens. Country B also grows wheat and corn, but exports most of it. When Country A discovers huge amounts of crude oil beneath those fields previously used to grow corn and wheat, it must decide what to do.
   Which of the following would give Country A comparative advantage? 2.____

   A. Devoting resources to extracting and exporting crude oil, and importing wheat and corn
   B. Continuing to grow its own wheat and corn
   C. Continuing to grow some wheat and corn, while exporting some oil
   D. Continuing to grow wheat and corn in order to export it

3. When a debtor can no longer meet financial obligations, he, she, or it must undergo this legal process in order to be relieved of those debts in order to start anew: 3.____

   A. breach of contract
   B. bankruptcy
   C. call provision
   D. criminal loss protection

4. The money left after a company distributes dividends to its stockholders is 4.____

   A. revenue
   B. profit
   C. net earnings
   D. retained earnings

5. The commercial law, adopted by every state, covering sales and commercial laws is called the 5.____

   A. Uniform Commercial Code
   B. Labor-Management Relations Act
   C. Federal Trade Commission Act
   D. General Agreement on Tariffs and Trade

6. A city, county, and/or state police force is an example of 6.____

   A. socialism
   B. public goods
   C. communism
   D. private goods

7. Funds raised within a company are considered 7.____

   A. debt capital
   B. revenue
   C. secured bonds
   D. equity capital

8. The StarDaze Lighting Company decides to order fewer glass orders with its glass supplier, due to a decline in sales. The glass supplier, in turn, lays off some of its workers, and those workers then have less money to spend on entertainment.
This chain of events is known as

   A. the business cycle
   B. the multiplier effect
   C. recession
   D. supply-side economics

9. An economic system in which all or most of the means of production are privately owned and operated for profit is called

   A. capitalism
   B. communism
   C. democracy
   D. socialism

10. During a time of economic growth, if the government acts to adjust interest rates in order to dampen the economy, its actions are an example of

    A. disinflation
    B. financial sabotage
    C. monetary policy
    D. fiscal policy

11. The value of one currency in comparison to currencies of other countries is called the _____ rate.

    A. discount
    B. exchange
    C. market
    D. federal funds

12. Which of the following factors contribute to inflation?

    A. Government borrowing
    B. Increase in the price of imported goods
    C. Unemployment
    D. All of the above

13. Two consecutive quarters of negative growth in the real GNP is called

    A. stagflation
    B. inflation
    C. depression
    D. recession

14. The value of using a resource, measured against the best alternative to using that resource is called

    A. opportunity cost
    B. scarcity of resources
    C. innovation
    D. profit motive

15. Which of the following is considered capital?

    A. Labor
    B. Natural resources
    C. Buildings used to produce goods and services
    D. All of the above

16. What is a trial balance?

    A. Purchasing goods now and paying for them later
    B. A summary of all data in the ledgers in order to test the accuracy of the figures
    C. A line of credit temporarily guaranteed by a bank
    D. A loan payable in a period of over one year

17. Products used to produce other products are called

    A. industrial goods
    B. negotiable instruments
    C. tangible assets
    D. support goods

18. Bill Johnson is a United States importer trading in a time when the United States dollar is weak in comparison to foreign currencies. What will be the impact of this on Johnson and other United States importers?

    A. Importers will likely form a trade barrier.
    B. There will be no impact because demand for imports is not price sensitive.
    C. Import sales will increase.
    D. Import sales will decrease.

19. The distribution strategy which uses one retail outlet in a given geographic area is called _____ distribution.

    A. corporate
    B. contractual
    C. exclusive
    D. intensive

20. Susan Williams owns a florist shop. She must decide whether to spend $500 on seasonal flowers for the holiday season and cut back on regular stock. Her choice is an example of

    A. opportunity cost
    B. innovation
    C. scarcity of resources
    D. profit motive

21. A promissory note which requires the borrower to repay the loan in specified installments is called a

    A. trade deficit
    B. long-term loan
    C. term loan agreement
    D. trade credit

22. Selling accounts receivable for cash is called

    A. hedging
    B. inventory financing
    C. pledging
    D. factoring

23. An entrepreneur who invests money and effort into producing a product, and then brings it to the market is exhibiting

    A. the profit motive
    B. opportunity cost
    C. the charity motive
    D. the quality motive

24. When a bank issues a note which earns a guaranteed interest for a fixed period of time, it is called a

    A. bond
    B. convertible bond
    C. certificate of deposit
    D. debenture bond

25. Which of the following is a DISADVANTAGE of a sole proprietorship?

    A. Strict government reporting requirements
    B. Difficulty with forming them
    C. Difficulties among partners
    D. Unlimited liability

4 (#1)

KEY (CORRECT ANSWERS)

1. C
2. A
3. B
4. D
5. A

6. B
7. D
8. B
9. A
10. D

11. B
12. D
13. D
14. A
15. C

16. B
17. A
18. D
19. C
20. A

21. C
22. D
23. A
24. C
25. D

———

TEST 2

DIRECTIONS: Each question or incomplete statement is followed by several suggested answers or completions. Select the one that BEST answers the question or completes the statement. *PRINT THE LETTER OF THE CORRECT ANSWER IN THE SPACE AT THE RIGHT.*

1. This type of unemployment results from people losing their jobs when their occupation is no longer part of the main structure of the economy. 1.____

   A. Structural
   B. Seasonal
   C. Frictional
   D. Cyclical

2. Which of the following is an example of an institutional investor? 2.____

   A. Individual investor in a mutual fund
   B. Voting stockholder
   C. Mutual fund
   D. Non-voting stockholder

3. When a manager acts as a resource allocator, what type of role is he/she fulfilling? 3.____

   A. Leadership
   B. Decision-making
   C. Informational
   D. Liaison

4. Which of the following steps are required for starting a partnership? 4.____
   I. Obtaining invoices and other business invoices
   II. Opening a checking account for business
   III. Creating a buy/sell agreement
   IV. Choosing a state in which to incorporate

   The CORRECT answer is:

   A. I, III, IV
   B. II, III, IV
   C. I, II, III
   D. I, II, III, IV

5. Which of the following is a middle-management position? 5.____

   A. CEO
   B. Supervisor
   C. Foreman
   D. Plant manager

6. The financial position of a firm at a specific date is reported on a(n) 6.____

   A. balance sheet
   B. bookkeeping ledger
   C. accounting report
   D. certificate of deposit

7. A consumer's right to be informed includes which of the following? 7.____

   A. The ability to be heard
   B. The ability to trust that a product is safe
   C. Knowing what is in a product
   D. The ability to choose between products

8. When employees, managers or investors attempt to purchase an organization through borrowing, it is called 8.____

   A. a leveraged buyout
   B. a hostile takeover
   C. a call provision
   D. buying on margin

9. Which of the following is an example of a product franchise?

    A. Coca-Cola bottling plant
    B. Car dealer
    C. Boston Chicken
    D. Shell gas station

10. The classical theory of motivation holds that _____ is the sole motivator in the workplace.

    A. fairness
    B. ethics
    C. success
    D. money

11. Government regulations limiting the import of goods and services in order to protect domestic producers is referred to as

    A. a primary boycott
    B. a protective tariff
    C. trade protectionism
    D. a closed-shop agreement

12. Which of the following is an employee-oriented motivational technique?

    A. Job sharing
    B. Flextime
    C. Job enrichment
    D. Behavior modification

13. This law forbids contracts, combinations or conspiracies in restraint of trade, monopolies or attempts to monopolize.

    A. Robinson-Patman Act
    B. Sherman Anti-Trust Act
    C. National Labor Relations Act
    D. General Agreement on Tariffs and Trade

14. The sale of part of a company is known as

    A. divestiture
    B. leveraged buyout
    C. merger
    D. hostile takeover

15. The law which prohibits any practice which will result in a monopoly is the

    A. Federal Trade Commission Act
    B. General Agreement on Tariffs and Trade
    C. Clayton Act
    D. Robinson-Patman Act

16. What is the most common fringe benefit provided by employers?

    A. Paid holidays
    B. Stock ownership
    C. Retirement benefits
    D. Insurance

17. _____ liability provides no legal defense for placing a product on the market that is dangerous to the consumer because of known or knowable defects.

    A. Unlimited
    B. Strict
    C. Limited
    D. Rule of indemnity

18. Trying to extend the life cycle of products by changing features of the product is called

    A. product differentiation
    B. market segmentation
    C. target marketing
    D. product modification

19. Which economic system grants the government the greatest degree of ownership and control?   19.____

    A. Socialism
    C. Communism
    B. Capitalism
    D. Modified capitalism

20. The distribution system which uses a preferred group of retailers in an area is called   20.____

    A. selective distribution
    C. exclusive distribution
    B. spot marketing
    D. the push strategy

21. Which of the following are among the most common forces of international business activity?   21.____

    I. Importing and exporting
    II. Tariffs and embargoes
    III. Licensing and franchising

    The CORRECT answer is:

    A. I, II   B. I, III   C. II, III   D. I, II, III

22. An owner in a business who has no management responsibility or liability for losses beyond the original investment is a   22.____

    A. chief financial officer (CFO)
    B. general partner
    C. limited partner
    D. small business entrepreneur

23. An economy which combines free markets with government allocation of some resources is a(n)   23.____

    A. mixed economy
    C. communist economy
    B. oligopoly
    D. capitalist economy

24. A corporation whose stock is owned entirely (or almost entirely) by another corporation is called a   24.____

    A. private corporation
    C. parent company
    B. professional corporation
    D. subsidiary corporation

25. A country with a monopoly on producing a product (or a country able to produce a product at a cost below that of all other countries) has a(n)   25.____

    A. oligopoly
    B. absolute advantage
    C. penetration strategy advantage
    D. absolute liability

KEY (CORRECT ANSWERS)

1. A
2. C
3. B
4. C
5. D

6. A
7. C
8. A
9. B
10. D

11. C
12. D
13. B
14. A
15. C

16. D
17. B
18. D
19. C
20. A

21. B
22. C
23. A
24. D
25. B

———

EXAMINATION SECTION
TEST 1

DIRECTIONS: Each question or incomplete statement is followed by several suggested answers or completions. Select the one that BEST answers the question or completes the statement. *PRINT THE LETTER OF THE CORRECT ANSWER IN THE SPACE AT THE RIGHT.*

1. Which of the following would PROBABLY be the long-term result if millions of citizens stopped saving and investing a part of their income?

    A. The rate of economic growth would decrease.
    B. The supply of economic goods would increase.
    C. Employment would decrease.
    D. The law of supply and demand would no longer apply.

2. Which of the following would a consumer generally contact FIRST to resolve a problem about a purchased product?

    A. A federal government consumer protection office
    B. The manufacturer of the product
    C. The firm from which the product was purchased
    D. The local Better Business Bureau

3. Which of the following is a MAJOR benefit of using credit? It

    A. lets people buy everything they want
    B. promotes efficient record-keeping
    C. permits the use of a product while paying for it
    D. provides an incentive for saving

4. Dave wants to be on the swim team. To participate, he would have to give up his part-time job.
   This situation BEST illustrates which of the following economic concepts?

    A. Opportunity costs   B. Economic interdependence
    C. Productive resources   D. Supply and demand

5. The total current market value of all goods and services produced during a year in the nation is called the

    A. national income
    B. national inventory
    C. gross national product
    D. national disposable income

6. A credit rating usually determines whether a person will be granted credit and how much credit will be granted. Which of the following practices could lead to a person being given a POOR credit rating?

    A. Paying bills in full when they are presented
    B. Failing to resolve billing errors or related problems
    C. Consulting creditors without delay if bills cannot be paid on time
    D. Using credit in such a way as to be able to repay without difficulty

7. One day, Anne could not decide which of five different-colored shirts to buy, so she bought one of each. Another day, she saw a jacket she liked in a store window and bought it. Later, she was notified that her checking account was overdrawn, and, unfortunately, she had not yet bought a birthday gift for a party the next day.
Anne's behavior indicates that she does not understand which of the following economic principles?

   A. Limited resources and unlimited wants necessitate choices and decisions.
   B. Increases in price affect purchases of goods.
   C. Increases in consumer demand affect supply and price.
   D. Individuals earn and spend income freely in a mixed economy.

8. Which of the following is a written statement signed by a buyer stating that the seller has the right to take back goods if the buyer does NOT pay for them? A(n)

   A. acceleration agreement
   B. security agreement
   C. wage-assignment agreement
   D. balloon clause

9. The MAIN reason for balancing a checking account is to determine

   A. whether deposits were correctly listed
   B. what the bank's service charges are
   C. which checks have been written
   D. whether bank and personal records agree

10. Which of the following is a MAJOR role of government in the economic system of the United States? To

    A. guarantee minimum earnings for all citizens
    B. compete with private enterprise in providing goods and services
    C. encourage the consumer to conserve resources
    D. make adjustments to the economy by regulating taxes and government spending

11. Which of the following is LEAST likely to influence an individual's income from employment?

    A. Relative demand for the occupation in which the individual is employed
    B. The degree of skill required for the job
    C. The amount of the individual's savings and investments
    D. The level of education attained

12.

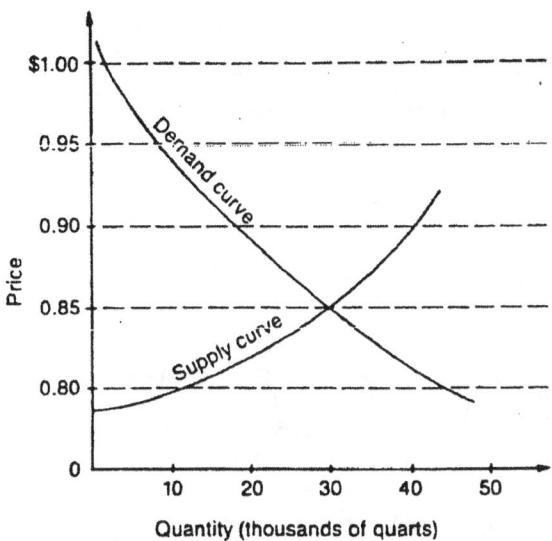

SUPPLY-DEMAND CURVE
FOR ORANGE JUICE

The market price is that price at which the producer (supplier) is willing to sell and the consumer (demander) is willing to buy.
Which of these is the market price for a quart of orange juice?

A. $0.80   B. $0.85   C. $0.90   D. $1.00

13. Which of the following legal channels is probably the BEST way to resolve a consumer dispute involving a limited amount of money?

A. Complaint to the Governor
B. Private lawsuit
C. Small claims court
D. Suit brought through the state Attorney General

14. If consumers do not pay the total amount owed on a department store charge account at the end of the month, they must pay all or part of the account balance plus an additional amount when making the next payment.
Which of the following MOST accurately describes the additional amount that is added to the account balance?

A. Monthly payment
C. Finance charge
B. Annual percentage rate
D. Yearly interest

15. If the supply of a good or service decreases and the demand stays the same, which of the following is MOST likely to occur first?
The price will _____ and the quantity demanded will _____ .

A. increase; decrease
C. decrease; increase
B. decrease; decrease
D. increase; increase

16. Which of the following foods could be substituted for meat and also provide a relatively low-cost, nutritious meal?

   A. Eggs
   B. Yellow vegetables
   C. Pasta
   D. Potatoes

17.

> YOUR GRADES WILL IMPROVE
>
> NO MORE MISSPELLED WORDS
>
> Over 5,000 of the world's most commonly misspelled words on a handy 11" x 17" chart.
>
> Send $3.00 plus $1.00 postage to:
>
> SPELL-RIGHT CHART
> P.O. Box 123
> Reading, MI 49274
>
> NO MORE CLUMSY DICTIONARIES!

Which of the following statements is a fact rather than an opinion?

   A. A chart user is unlikely to make spelling errors again.
   B. It costs $4.00 to order the chart.
   C. A chart user will no longer need a dictionary.
   D. Grades will improve with the use of the chart.

18. Ms. Lopez has $1,000 that she does not intend to spend at this time. Which of the following actions would assure her access to her money whenever she needs it?

   A. Deposit it in a passbook savings account at an insured commercial bank or an insured savings and loan association.
   B. Buy gold through a commodities broker.
   C. Purchase term life insurance through an insurance broker.
   D. Buy common stock through a reputable brokerage firm.

19. Which of the following magazines is generally considered the BEST source of reliable information about product testing and product ratings?

   A. WALL STREET JOURNAL
   B. MONEY
   C. CONSUMER REPORTS
   D. NEWSWEEK

20. Which of the following will have the GREATEST influence on the cost of insurance provided by an insurance company? The

   A. company's estimate of the risk involved
   B. number of agents employed by the company
   C. policyholders' ability to pay premiums
   D. dollar volume of the company's business

KEY (CORRECT ANSWERS)

1.	A	11.	C
2.	C	12.	B
3.	C	13.	C
4.	A	14.	C
5.	C	15.	A
6.	B	16.	A
7.	A	17.	B
8.	B	18.	A
9.	D	19.	C
10.	C	20.	A

TEST 2

DIRECTIONS: Each question or incomplete statement is followed by several suggested answers or completions. Select the one that BEST answers the question or completes the statement. *PRINT THE LETTER OF THE CORRECT ANSWER IN THE SPACE AT THE RIGHT.*

1. Which health care insurance would probably be the LEAST expensive for most elderly people?

    A. A group insurance plan
    B. An individual policy from an insurance company
    C. Self-insuring through a savings program
    D. A family policy from an independent agent

1.____

2. Which information on a cereal package is there for the specific purpose of giving the nutritional quality?

    A. List of ingredients
    B. Net weight and price
    C. Recommended uses and recipes
    D. Percentage of recommended daily allowances

2.____

3. Which of the following is characteristic of a long-term, fixed-rate mortgage loan? The

    A. monthly payments are based on the consumer price index
    B. interest rate and monthly payments remain the same throughout the term of the loan
    C. interest rate of the loan is set by law
    D. monthly payments are automatically adjusted as the prime interest rate changes

3.____

4. In which of the following ways can people put their clothing dollars to BEST use?

    A. Buy clothes at the beginning of the seasons when new fashions are most plentiful in the stores.
    B. Consider needs and the amount of money available and then compare prices, quality, and fit.
    C. Select clothes that improve self-image without regard to the cost.
    D. Avoid sales because most sale clothes are leftovers and are rarely of good quality.

4.____

5. In MOST states, a tenant of rental property is required to

    A. agree not to sublet the property without permission
    B. make needed repairs to the property
    C. pay fire insurance premiums on the property and personal belongings
    D. make improvements that will then belong to the owner

5.____

6. Which of the following is generally NOT considered a reliable way to do comparison shopping?

    A. Telephoning various stores to check prices
    B. Checking newspaper advertisements
    C. Going from store to store to check prices
    D. Buying in a store recommended by a neighbor

6.____

7. If the sales tax is 4%, what is the TOTAL cost to the consumer of a $3.90 book? 7.____

   A. $4.26   B. $4.06   C. $5.66   D. $3.96

Questions 8-9.

DIRECTIONS: Questions 8 and 9 are based on the information below.

```
              THE JONES BUDGET
            (Net Monthly Income $1800)
                              PERCENTAGE
   ITEMS CATEGORY              OF BUDGET
   Clothing                        8%
   Food                           21%
   Housing                        33%
   Miscellaneous                  10%
   Savings                         7%
   Transportation                 21%
```

8. How much does the Jones family budget per month for miscellaneous expenses? 8.____

   A. $20   B. $17   C. $180   D. $185

9. For which of the following does the Jones family budget the GREATEST dollar amount per month? 9.____

   A. Clothing and miscellaneous
   B. Housing
   C. Food
   D. Transportation

10. Which of the following statements about income from employment is the MOST accurate? 10.____

    A. Clerical and service workers earn about the same amount as craftworkers.
    B. Union members generally earn more than nonunion members doing the same job.
    C. Women's earnings are comparable to men's earnings throughout their working lives.
    D. High school graduates and those with an eighth-grade education earn about the same amount.

11. Laura wants to buy a used car. 11.____
    Which of the following would assure her the BEST chance of buying a car in good operating condition?

    A. Buying the car from a friend or neighbor
    B. Testdriving the car herself
    C. Buying the car from a new car dealer
    D. Having a certified mechanic inspect the car

12. In theory, a progressive income tax is one whereby all citizens 12.____

    A. contribute the same percentage of their income
    B. are taxed, but businesses are not
    C. pay less as the amount of base income increases
    D. pay according to their ability

13. At what point is it no longer worthwhile to do research about the product before making a purchase? The

    A. research costs begin to exceed probable benefits
    B. transportation costs for comparison shopping begin to increase
    C. information search leads to confusion over the variety of choices
    D. time spent in the library is felt to be pleasant but nonproductive.

14. A lease is BEST defined as a(n)

    A. agreement between a landlord and a tenant
    B. agreement between the seller of a house and the buyer
    C. warranty that a property is in good condition
    D. statement of a tenant's credit standing

15. When many firms compete to produce one type of product, which of the following will PROBABLY happen?

    A. It will be hard for a new firm to enter the market for that product.
    B. People will remain loyal to the brand they have been using.
    C. There will be improvements in the quality of the product.
    D. Prices will rise because competition leads to increased production costs.

16. Which of the following would USUALLY be considered a fraud committed by consumers against business?

    A. Making complaints about service
    B. Applying for refunds
    C. Declaring bankruptcy
    D. Returning goods after using them

17. Which of the following BEST describes take-home pay as opposed to gross pay? The

    A. amount of pay left after all deductions are made
    B. total family income from all sources
    C. gross pay plus a cost-of-living allowance
    D. hourly pay rate times the number of hours worked

18. Which of the following sales schemes allows a person to earn a rebate or commission by providing the names of friends or relatives and recommending the product to them?

    A. Buying club   B. Bait-and-switch
    C. Chain referral   D. Mail fraud

19. If consumers decide that product A and product B are equivalent, they will usually base their decision to purchase product A or product B PRIMARILY on

    A. the comparative prices of product A and product B
    B. the attractiveness of the packaging of the two products
    C. their desire to keep the producers of both product A and product B in business
    D. the amount of advertising for the two products'

20. The reason generally given for buying life insurance is to 20.____
    A. get a tax deduction for premiums paid
    B. supplement pension income and social security payments
    C. protect dependents of the insured in case of the insured's death
    D. protect savings from inflation

KEY (CORRECT ANSWERS)

1.	A	11.	D
2.	D	12.	D
3.	B	13.	A
4.	B	14.	A
5.	A	15.	C
6.	D	16.	D
7.	B	17.	A
8.	C	18.	C
9.	B	19.	A
10.	B	20.	C

EXAMINATION SECTION
TEST 1

DIRECTIONS: Each question or incomplete statement is followed by several suggested answers or completions. Select the one that BEST answers the question or completes the statement. *PRINT THE LETTER OF THE CORRECT ANSWER IN THE SPACE AT THE RIGHT.*

1. Companies with successful customer service organizations usually experience each of the following EXCEPT
   A. fewer customer complaints
   B. greater response to advertising
   C. lower marketing costs
   D. more repeat business

   1._____

2. To be most useful to an organization, feedback received from customers should be each of the following EXCEPT
   A. centered on internal customers
   B. orgoing
   C. focused on a limited number of indicators
   D. available to every employee in the organization

   2._____

3. Instead of directly saying *no* to a customer, service representatives will usually get BEST results with a reply that begins with the words:
   A. I'll try
   B. I don't believe
   C. You can
   D. It's not our policy

   3._____

4. Once a customer problem is identified, each of the following should become a part of the service recovery process EXCEPT
   A. following up on the problem resolution
   B. making whatever promises are necessary
   C. providing the customer with what was originally requested
   D. listening and responding to every complaint given by the customer

   4._____

5. The percentage of an organization's annual business that involves repeat customers is CLOSEST to
   A. 25%   B. 45%   C. 65%   D. 85%

   5._____

6. Of the following, the _____ is NOT generally considered to be a major source of *service promise*.
   A. customer service representative
   B. organization
   C. particular department that delivers product to the customer
   D. customer

   6._____

7. A customer appears to be mildly irritated when lodging a complaint. The MOST appropriate action for a service representative to take while attempting resolution is to
   A. allow venting of frustrations
   B. enlist the customer in generating solutions
   C. show emotional neutrality
   D. create calm

8. If an organization loses one customer who normally spends $50 per week, the projected result of reduction in sales for the following year will be APPROXIMATELY
   A. $2,600   B. $12,400   C. $124,000   D. $950,000

9. The majority of *service promises* originate from
   A. organizational management
   B. customer service professionals
   C. the customers' expectations
   D. organizational marketing

10. To arrive at a *fair fix* to a service problem, one should FIRSTS
    A. offer an apology for the problem
    B. ask probing questions to understand and confirm the nature of the problem
    C. listen to the customer's description of the problem
    D. determine and implement a solution to the problem

11. Which of the following is NOT generally considered to be a function of *open questioning* when dealing with a customer?
    A. Defining problems
    B. Confirming an order
    C. Getting more information
    D. Establishing customer needs

12. When dealing with a customer, service representatives should generally use the pronoun
    A. *they*, meaning the company as a whole
    B. *they*, meaning the department to whom the complaint will be referred
    C. *I*, meaning themselves, as representatives of the organization
    D. *we*, meaning themselves and the customer

13. A customer service representative demonstrates product and service knowledge by
    A. anticipating the changing needs of customers
    B. soliciting feedback from customers about customer service
    C. studying the capabilities of the office computer system
    D. knowing what questions are asked most by customers about a product or service

14. When listening to a customer during a face-to-face meeting, the MOST appropriate non-verbal gesture is
    A. clenched fists
    B. leaning slightly toward a customer
    C. hands casually in pockets
    D. standing with crossed arms

15. Before breaking or bending an existing service rule in order to better serve a customer, a representative should be aware of each of the following EXCEPT the
    A. reason for the rule
    B. location of a written copy of the rule and policy
    C. consequences of not following the rule
    D. situations in which the rule is applicable

16. The LEAST likely reason for a dissatisfied customer's failure to complain about a product or service is that the customer
    A. does not think the complaint will produce the desired results
    B. is unaware of the proper channels through which to voice his/her complaint
    C. does not believe he/she has the time to spend on the complaint
    D. does not believe anyone in the organization really cares about the complaint

17. Most research shows that _____% of what is communicated between people during face-to-face meetings is conveyed through entirely nonverbal cues.
    A. 10   B. 30   C. 50   D. 80

18. When a customer submits a written complaint, the representative should write a response that avoids
    A. addressing every single component of the customer's complaint
    B. a personal tone
    C. the use of a pre-formulated response structure
    D. mentioning future business transactions

19. A customer service representative spends several hours practicing with the various forms and paperwork required by the company for handling customer service situations.
    Which of the following basic areas of learning is the representative trying to improve upon?
    A. Interpersonal skills
    B. Product and service knowledge
    C. Customer knowledge
    D. Technical skills

20. If a customer service representative must deal with other members of a service team in order to resolve a problem, the representative should avoid
    A. developing personal relationships
    B. giving others credit for ideas that clearly were not theirs
    C. circumventing uncooperative team members by quietly contacting a superior
    D. involving customers in the resolution of a complaint

21. A customer service representative is willing to help customers promptly.
    Which of the following service factors is the representative able to demonstrate?
    A. Assurance
    B. Responsiveness
    C. Empathy
    D. Reliability

22. A service representative begins work in a specialized order entry job and son learns that many customers call in with orders at the last minute, causing her routine to be thrown out of balance and creating stress.
After studying the ordering patterns of all clients, the MOST effective resolution to the problem would be to
   A. mail reminder notices to habitually late customers in advance of typical ordering dates to establish lead time
   B. telephone habitually late customers a few days before their typical ordering dates to establish lead time
   C. place the orders of habitually late customers in advance, changing them later if necessary
   D. establish and enforce a rigid lead-time deadline to create more manageable client behavior

22.____

23. For BEST results, customer service representatives will improve service by considering themselves to be representative of
   A. the entire organization
   B. the department receiving the complaint
   C. the customer
   D. an adversary of the organization, who will fight along with the customer

23.____

24. Of all the customers who stop doing business with organizations, ____% do so because of product dissatisfaction.
   A. 15   B. 40   C. 65   D. 80

24.____

25. When using the *problem-solving* approach to solve the problem of a dissatisfied customer, the LAST step should be to
   A. double check for customer satisfaction
   B. identify the customer's expectations
   C. outline a solution or alternatives
   D. take action on the problem

25.____

KEY (CORRECT ANSWERS)

1.	B	11.	B
2.	A	12.	C
3.	C	13.	D
4.	B	14.	B
5.	C	15.	B
6.	C	16.	C
7.	B	17.	C
8.	A	18.	C
9.	B	19.	D
10.	C	20.	C

21. B
22. B
23. A
24. A
25. A

TEST 2

DIRECTIONS: Each question or incomplete statement is followed by several suggested answers or completions. Select the one that BEST answers the question or completes the statement. *PRINT THE LETTER OF THE CORRECT ANSWER IN THE SPACE AT THE RIGHT.*

1. Of the following, the LEAST likely reason for a customer to telephone an organization or department is to
   A. voice an objection
   B. make a statement
   C. offer praise
   D. ask a question

   1.____

2. Customer service usually requires each of the following EXCEPT
   A. product knowledge
   B. friendliness and approachability
   C. problem-solving skills
   D. company/organization knowledge

   2.____

3. According to research, a typical dissatisfied customer will tell about _____ people how dissatisfied he/she is with an organization's product or service.
   A. 3   B. 5   C. 10   D. 20

   3.____

4. When a service target is provided by manager, it is MOST important for a service representative to know the
   A. nature of the customer database associated with the target
   B. formula for achieving the target
   C. methods used by other service personnel for achieving the target
   D. purpose behind the target

   4.____

5. Typically, customers cause about _____ of the service and product problems they complain about.
   A. 1/5   B. 1/3   C. 1/2   D. 2/3

   5.____

6. When a dissatisfied customer complains to a service representative, making a sale is NOT considered to be good service when the
   A. customer appreciates being changed to a different service or product
   B. the original product or service is in need of additional parts or components to be complete
   C. the customer remains angry about the original complaint
   D. the original product or service is in need of repair

   6.____

7. As service representatives, personnel would be LEAST likely to be responsible for
   A. service
   B. marketing
   C. problem-solving
   D. sales

   7.____

8. When writing a memorandum on a customer complaint, _____ can be considered optional by a service representative.
   A. the date the complaint was filed and/or the problem occurred
   B. a summary of the customer's comments
   C. the address of the customer
   D. a suggestion for correcting the situation

   8.____

9. In most successful organizations, customer service is considered PRIMARILY to be the domain of the
   A. entire organization
   B. sales department
   C. complaint department
   D. service department

10. According to MOST research, the cost of attracting a new customer, in relation to the cost of retaining a current customer, is about
    A. half as much
    B. about the same
    C. twice as much
    D. five times as much

11. If a customer service representative is unable to do what a customer asks, the representative should avoid
    A. quoting organizational policy regarding the customer's request
    B. explaining why it cannot be done
    C. making specific statements
    D. offering alternatives

12. When a customer presents a service representative with a request, the representative's FIRST reaction should usually be a(n)
    A. apology
    B. friendly greeting
    C. statement of organizational policy regarding the request
    D. request for clarifying information

13. It is NOT a primary reason for written communication with customers to
    A. create documentation
    B. solidify relationships
    C. confirm understanding
    D. solicit business contact

14. Of the following, which would be LEAST frustrating for a customer to hear from a service representative?
    A. You will have to
    B. I will do my best
    C. Let me see what I can do
    D. He/she should be back any minute

15. A customer appears to be mildly irritated when lodging a complaint. It is MOST appropriate for a service representative to demonstrate _____ in reaction to the complaint.
    A. urgency
    B. empathy
    C. nonchalance
    D. surprise

16. The _____ would be indirectly served by an individual who takes customer orders at an organization's telephone center.
    A. customer
    B. management personnel
    C. billing agents
    D. warehouse staff

17. Based on the actions of a customer service representative, customers will be MOST likely to make judgments concerning each of the following EXCEPT the
    A. kind of people employed by the organization
    B. company's value system
    C. organization's commitment to advertised promises
    D. value of the organization's product

18. When dealing with customers, a service representative's apologies, if necessary, should NOT be
    A. immediate B. official C. sincere D. personal

19. Of all the customers who stop doing business with organizations, approximately _____ do so because of indifferent treatment by employees.
    A. 20% B. 45% C. 70% D. 95%

20. If a customer service representative is aware that the organization is not capable of meeting a customer's expectations, the representative's FIRST responsibility would be to
    A. tell the customer of the organization's inability to comply
    B. shape the customer's expectations to match what the organization can do as he/she asks
    C. encourage the customer to believe that the organization can do as he/she asks
    D. make the sale on the organization's product

21. The following is an example of a *bonus benefit* associated with a product or service:
    A customer
    A. buys a sporty sedan and finds that its tight turning ratio makes it easy to park
    B. buys bread specifically because he wants to receive a coupon for his next purchase
    C. purchases a car and discovers a strange smell in the upholstery
    D. buys a music audiotape and discovers that there are advertisements at the beginning and end of the tape

22. Approximately _____ of customers who voice complaints with an organization will continue to do business with the organization if the complaint is resolved promptly.
    A. 25 B. 40 C. 75 D. 95

23. Though necessary, a positive, proactive customer satisfaction policy will USUALLY be restricted by costs and
    A. volume of service problems
    B. limitations of management personnel authority
    C. unreasonable customer demands
    D. limitations of service policy

24. According to MOST customers, _____ prevents good listening on the part of a service representative when a customer is speaking.
    A. technological apparatus (e.g., voicemail)
    B. frequent interruptions by other staff or customers
    C. asking unnecessary questions
    D. background noise

25. The ability to provide the promised service or product dependably and accurately maybe defined as
    A. assurance
    B. responsiveness
    C. courtesy
    D. reliability

25._____

KEY (CORRECT ANSWERS)

1. C
2. B
3. C
4. D
5. B

6. C
7. B
8. C
9. A
10. D

11. A
12. D
13. D
14. C
15. A

16. B
17. D
18. B
19. C
20. B

21. A
22. D
23. D
24. B
25. D

BASIC FUNDAMENTALS OF EFFECTIVE ADVERTISING

I. INTRODUCTION

Just as sales are the life blood of a business, advertising and sales promotion are the transfusions that keep sales alive and active and the business profitable. Advertising and sales promotion are, of course, parts of the same effort. But because of our limited time, we will speak only of advertising in this presentation—reserving discussion of sales promotion for another time.

Never has advertising been a more vital tool to managers of small business than it is today. The finest product or service is useless until it is in the hands of a consumer or user. Inventories, as long as they remain on your shelves or in your stock bins, are not a profit but an investment--an element of expense.

In our highly competitive economy, business success depends on the sales that are rung up on the thousands of cash registers across the land. The cash register is the focal point of the business, and you don't make a nickel until its bell rings.

The postwar years in the United States have witnessed the greatest material prosperity ever known to man. And the years ahead promise even greater growthif we can accelerate consumer buying. This is the reasoning behind Government attempts to increase the purchase of consumer goods by releasing more consumer buying power. Aside from political or purely statistical considerations, the fact remains that as a Nation we must increase our consumer sales if we are to maintain today's living standard for our increasing population.

II. ROLE OF ADVERTISING

Most people must be motivated to want before they will buy. And advertising is our mass motivator.

When you greet the customer who enters your place of business, you are advertising. When you display an item of merchandise in your showroom instead of storing it in your stockroom, you are advertising. And when Mrs. Smith tells Mrs. Jones about the wonderful service you offer, that's advertising of the most valuable kind.

Yet word-of-mouth advertising and point-of-sale advertising, such as these examples, are slow and, to a degree, unpredictable. To increase sales, we must accelerate the means of motivation. Many times, the difference between point-of-sale and mass advertising is as great as the difference between creeping and running. And we must run, and run fast, if we are to succeed in our goal.

Whether a business organization should advertise is no longer questioned. Now, we ask, "How much? " and "What kind? "

III. ADVERTISING HAS POWER

The old saying, "Build a better mousetrap and the world will beat a path to your door," no longer holds true. The businessman of today must be able to overcome resistance, inertia, and competitive claims. Advertising can be that magnetic force.

A. Drawing Power

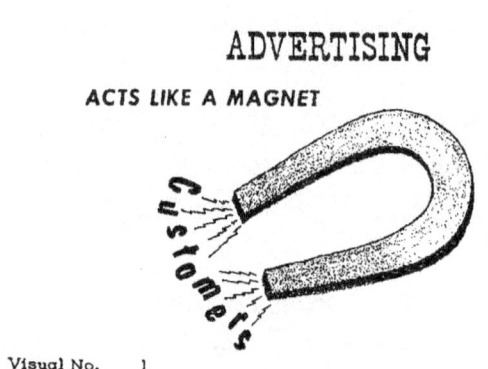

Visual No. 1

Let's use a magnet to illustrate this drawing power. The magnet represents your business and the high degree of internal pulling power it has because of the quality of your products and the nature or caliber of your services. A handful of steel shavings representing potential customers-sprinkled around but slightly removed from the magnet- would give us the situation of a business with a certain amount of pulling power within an area of potential trade. Very little happens because the internal pulling power of the magnet or business is not enough in itself to draw customers.

But if we attach a couple of steel rods to the poles of the magnet, the shavings (or customers) will immediately cluster around the steel rods. The rods, in effect, have extended the internal pulling power of the magnet itself.

In a business, the arms that extend the internal drawing power and reach out to mass markets are the arms of sales promotion and advertising. By means of their drawing power, customers are attracted to the business.

Recently a linoleum maker's survey found that 80 percent of the people interested in using linoleum (not just for kitchens, but for other areas of the home such as halls, play rooms, dining rooms, and so forth) could not give the name of a single retail store where they could buy it. What a tremendous potential of prospects not yet tied to a competitor!

B. Holding Power

But what about those businessmen who are satisfied with the status quo, the volume of business they're now doing? Fortunately, there aren't many because no business can stand still for long. It must do better or it will do worse. It must grow or it will diminish. It must attract new customers because the market itself is in a constant state of flux. Consumer tastes and loyalties change, people are continually moving into or away from a trade area. An older generation dies or retires and a younger one takes its place. In other words, we might go back to our magnet example and say that in addition to having "drawing power," advertising has "holding power." Even if you don't want more business, you do want to protect what you already have. Stop advertising and what happens?

The National Retail Merchants Association estimates that the average store would have to go out of business in 3 or 4 years if it did no advertising because the average store loses between 20 and 25 percent of its customers each year, and these must be replaced just to maintain the status quo. This means that if you have 1,200 customers, you must add one customer a day to replace the one you lose.

Or consider the following trademarks. They represent products or services that led the American market less than a generation ago. Today, they are mostly forgotten because these products are no longer advertised--for one reason or another. Now let's take a look at a second set representing products that came upon the American scene about the same time as those we have just seen. They are very much alive today, and a part of that life they owe to the holding power of continued advertising.

Visual No. 2

These examples illustrate advertising's two top objectives: to draw in new customers, and to help hold old ones.

Advertising can also identify a business with the goods or service it offers.

It can build confidence in a business.

It can create good will.

It can increase sales and speed turnover.

It can reduce your expenses by spreading them over a larger volume.

Visual No. 3

However, there are a number of things advertising cannot do.

1. Advertising can't make a business prosper if that business offers only a poor product or an inferior kind of service.

2. Advertising can't lead to sales if the prospects which it brings in are ignored or poorly treated.

3. Advertising can't create traffic overnight, or increase sales with a single ad. (Unfortunately, many smaller businesses follow this kind of touch-and-go advertising policy.)

Visual No. 4

4. Advertising that is untruthful or misleading will not build confidence in the business that sponsors it.

1. The average independent store draws customers from not more than a quarter of a mile.

2. The average chain store draws customers from not more than three quarters of a mile.

3. The average shopping center draws customers from as far away as four miles.

When you advertise outside your market, all you're buying is waste coverage. So here are the things you should know:

Who are your customers or potential customers?

What income groups are they in?

Why do they buy? (Home or office, price or quality? On recommendation, or through advertising?)

How do they buy? (Cash or charge; do they want discounts? How often do they buy; what quantities?)

Where do they live? (In the neighborhood, or some distance from the store?)

How do they like your facilities, products, service?

It is also important to analyze your best, next best, and poorest prospects in your market area. Doing this will inform you about sales possibilities, the buying habits and the ability to buy of people in your market area, and basic trends in your market area. Knowing these factors gives you a sounder basis for developing selling and advertising appeals and selecting media.

V. DO YOU SELL PRICE OR QUALITY?

If low price is the basis of your business, then advertise price. Don't waste your money on pretty pictures, and don't be modest. Price advertising attracts price-conscious customers. If you cater to this group, talk their language.

If your business is patterned on quality, two main types of advertising are open to you, and you'll probably want to do some of each.

First, you'll want to tell people about:

1. New quality products or improved designs that you are offering.

2. Fresh, varied, and prestige stock or services.

3. Occasional sales for:

    A. Anniversaries or special occasions.
    B. Discontinued lines or remnant stock.
    C. New business development.

Second, you may want to advertise yourself and your organization rather than its products. This is called institutional advertising. The name sounds stuffy, but the advertising needn't be and shouldn't be.

With institutional advertising you can either be very dull and waste a lot of money, or you can do some of the most interesting, effective, and customer-producing advertising that a business can command. In institutional advertising you should emphasize:

4. Your years in business in the community.

5. Important jobs you have done.

6. The prestige of your service.

But remember: In advertising, say only one thing at a time. Choose the major point you want to make, and make it as effectively as you can. In other words, if the story you've chosen to tell is worth the telling, don't dilute it by mixing in a second or third one at the same time. If you try to feature everything in the same ad, you'll end up by featuring nothing.

VI. Name Brands and Product Advertising

You can give your advertising dollar a running start when you feature nationally advertised products or services, materials, equipment, etc. Manufacturers spend millions of dollars annually to advertise their products. By using these brand names and symbols in your own promotion, you can associate your firm with this national

You can see that advertising is one of your most important budget items because it attracts to your place of business the shoppers and customers who make it possible for you to meet your expenses and make a profit.

VIII. ADVERTISING APPEALS

To under stand the job your advertising will have to do, you must look beyond material features or the obvious and search out the intangible appeals that cause people to buy. People don't buy things--they buy goods that satisfy their wants. Every product or service that is marketable has some benefit that the potential customer must see and want before you can ring up a sale.

<u>People Buy Want-Satisfaction</u>

A toothpaste maker uses these appeals:

It helps to remove dingy film.
It penetrates crevices.
It washes away food particles.
It cleans and beautifies the teeth.

A motor oil refiner uses these:

It gives a motor pep and power.
It provides a quicker get-away.
It dissolves sludge, carbon, and motor varnish.
It saves up to 15 percent in gas and oil.
It frees sticky valves and rings.

IX. <u>Things People Want</u>

Peoples' wants are fairly standard. Most will react to one or another of the following appeals:
Convenience or comfort.
Love or friendship.
Desire for security.
Social approval or status.
Life, health, and well being.
Profit. savings, or economy.
Stylishness.

D. <u>Positioning</u>

Getting a good spot for your ad is desirable, but not always possible. Only rarely can you get a guarantee for a specific location, but you can usually arrange to have your ad appear on a certain page or in a given section. Occasionally, you may find your ad at the bottom of the page or next to an ad of your major competitor. It's important, therefore, to depend more on layout, design, and copy than to rely on a specific location. Always try to design your ad so that it won't be lost in the maze of an advertising page.

Some hints that may help you get better space treatment:

Visual No. 8

1. Don't quibble about insignificant details.

2. Write or type your copy plainly and without mistakes.

3. Handin your copy well before publication deadlines.

4. Don't ask for last-minute changes-- except in rare emergencies.

5. Pay your bill promptly. (Frequently, newspapers offer a significant discount for immediate payment.)

E. <u>Classified Ads</u>

Before we move on to discuss other types of advertising, let's consider classified as contrasted with display advertising.

1. Most people use the classified pages to look for specific items or services at featured prices.

2. Merchandise that is a special value and that makes for "consumer bargains" is readily sold through classified ads.

3. Closing-out of discontinued lines or old models of major and minor household appliances is readily handled through classified ads.

I. <u>Direct Mail Ads</u>

Direct mail has many of the advantages of handbills, and it is also a bit more dignified and personal because it can be directed to an individual customer.

Direct mail is more selective than newspaper, radio-TV, or handbills. To insure adequate but controlled coverage, use a selective mailing list compiled from your own business records or from various sources in your community. (Instructor will probably want to give local examples.) Telephone and city residence directories are also useful for this purpose.

Direct mail is somewhat more expensive than handbill advertising, but it will give you greater latitude because:

1. You can say more.

2. You can try novel ideas on selected clients.

3. You have a better chance to get across your business "personality."

4. You can use a more personal approach and appeal.

In addition to promotional sales letters and postal cards, direct mail advertising also includes stuffers to go into other mail (for example, bills). Using stuffers can save you quite a bit on postage.

IX. ADVERTISING AND TYPE OF BUSINESS

Your advertising program will depend on your type of business:

- If you have a quality, nonpromotional business (for example, an exclusive luggage shop), your advertising budget should be largely devoted to regular-priced merchandise advertising and to institutional, or prestige, advertising. You will need large amounts of clearance advertising, however, at the end of selling periods or seasons in order to get rid of slow movers and make way for new goods.
- If you have a semipromotional business (for example, a ladies high-fashion shoe salon), the largest share of your advertising will go to pushing regular-priced lines, but you will also need a sizable sum for special promotion advertising covering traditional sales events. If you have a well-rounded advertising program, you will have only an occasional need for clearance advertising.
- If you have a promotional business (for example, a discount appliance shop), the bulk of your comparatively large advertising budget will be applied to the special promotions that you depend on for large, immediate volume. You will seldom find it worthwhile to spend money on institutional advertising, except when you want to stress the policies you follow which make low prices possible. Promotional businesses require relatively little clearance advertising.

Each business has an image it presents to the community and its customers:

THE IMAGE OF A BUSINESS

CHEAP ...VS... EXPENSIVE
NEAT ...VS... SLOPPY
THOUGHTFUL ...VS... INDIFFERENT
HIGH INTEGRITY ...VS... QUESTIONABLE METHODS
FRIENDLY ...VS... IMPERSONAL

It can be "cheap" or "expensive"

It can be "neat" or "sloppy"

It can be "thoughtful" or "indifferent"

It can have "high integrity" or use "questionable methods"

It can be "warm and friendly" or "cold and impersonal"

Visual No. 10

These are several of the possibilities; you'll note that in each instance the image is created by your advertising, the appearance of your business, store, or office, and by you and your employees.

No matter what type of business you have, without customers you have nothing. So spend the money you need to get them and to meet your goals. Don't chisel on your advertising budget.

XII. DOES ADVERTISING PAY ITS WAY?

Effective advertising should pay you dividends, in the form of greater sales volume, in proportion to the amount of money you spend on it.

1. Your additional dollars of sales volume should total enough to pay for the advertising and the merchandise, operating expense, and net profit on your sales.
2. The amount of money you plan to put into advertising should be based on the business objective you hope to achieve, the type of business you have, and the medium you decide is the most economical for reaching your particular goals effectively.

A. Your Advertising Budget

Promotion is a part of your operating expense, and you should budget it just as you would other expenses. In order to avoid overspending or underspending, set up an advertising budget that can be used as an effective policy guide.

1. Include the expense of advertising in your markup calculations.

2. Put a definite amount into your operating budget to cover the cost of promotion.

   a. Find out the national averages of advertising percentages to sales ratios for your type of business.

   b. Adjust them to your local situations or conditions.

3. Make provisions in your budget for:

   a. The time or duration of your advertising program.

   b. The size, type, and layout of the ads you intend to use.

   c. The media you plan to use.

4. Check your budget periodically to be sure that your policy is getting results and that your estimated expenses were realistic.

XIII. GEAR ADVERTISING TO SALES GOAL

The first step you must take in planning an effective advertising campaign is to decide what you want advertising to do for you. Let's suppose, for example, that you have a dry cleaning business, that currently your sales volume is $50,000 a year, and that you want to double it within the next 5 years. Next year, then, you would need a volume of $60,000. After carefully considering all the factors that might determine the amount of money you could spend on advertising, suppose you decide that $750 would be about right. By dividing $750 by the planned sales volume of $60,000, you will find that the proposed advertising budget is equal to 1.25 percent of sales.

Most successful dry cleaners of your size spend between 2 and 3 percent of sales for advertising; thus the proposed $750 expenditure would appear to be far short of the amount needed for the growth you expect. You would have to spend about twice that much just to keep from falling behind competition, and perhaps even more to aid in any planned expansion. If you can't afford to spend about $2,000 for advertising, your hopes for doubling your sales in 5 years are probably too optimistic.

The size of your advertising budget should be determined by both your long-range and immediate sales objectives, and by comparison with the amount spent in other businesses. Although the proportion of income spent on advertising varies with the type of retail establishment, the average is roughly 1.5 percent.

XIV. <u>Measuring the Quality of an Ad</u>

Your advertising, like any other part of your business operation, must be frequently checked to determine if you are getting your money's worth from your advertising dollar. As far as results are concerned, any given piece of advertising can be good or bad. In advertising, there is no middle ground of indifference; an indifferent ad is a bad ad. You can run a special on seconds or salvaged merchandise, but not on poorly advertised merchandise.

You must always, therefore, judge each piece of advertising in terms of its qualities and effects as well as its cost.

<u>Qualities of a Good Ad</u>

1. Simple.
2. Informative.
3. Enthusiastic.
4. Truthful.
5. "Talks" to the reader about himself or his interests.
6. Tells a complete story without being tiring.
7. Emphasizes important features that are not evident.
8. ' Provides essential answers about who, what, when, where, how, and why.

Visual No. 11

11

Effects of a Good Ad

Visual No. 12

1. Gets favorable attention.

2. Creates interest.

3. Fans desire.

4. Stimulates action.

These observations we have been making can be summed up in one quick statement: "26 mountains in the State of Colorado are higher than Pikes Peak--but that's the one we know about!"

XV. HANDLING YOUR OWN ADVERTISING OR USING OUTSIDE HELP

There is no pat answer to whether you should handle your own advertising or use outside help. Too many variables are concerned: the size and nature of your business, the kind of market you want to reach, the sales volume you hope to produce. Besides, either/or questions can be misleading; sometimes you may need professional

www.ingramcontent.com/pod-product-compliance
Lightning Source LLC
Chambersburg PA
CBHW082041300426
44117CB00015B/2560